CORE CURRICULUM COURSE

Copyright © 2020 Wendy Bowen

ALL RIGHTS RESERVED WORLDWIDE

ISBN: 978-1-951280-09-3

MANIFEST
PUBLICATIONS

Unless otherwise noted, Scripture taken from the HOLY BIBLE, NEW INTERNATIONAL VERSION ® NIV ® Copyright © 1973, 1978, 1984, 2011 by Biblica, Inc. Used by permission of Biblica, Inc. All rights reserved worldwide. – Scripture quotations are taken from the Holy Bible, New Living Translation, copyright © 1996, 2004, 2007 by Tyndale House Foundation. Used by permission of Tyndale House Publishers, Inc. Carol Stream, Illinois 60188. All rights reserved. – Scripture taken from the New King James Version ®. Copyright © 1982 by Thomas Nelson, Inc. Used by permission. All rights reserved.
If other translations have unintentionally been included in this assembly without proper indication, please forgive me.

DEDICATION

To Jesus, the One who promises that if we seek first His Kingdom and His righteousness, all things will be added unto us and that if we delight ourselves in Him, He will give us the desires of our heart.
– Matthew 6:33, Psalm 37:4

...Because You always fulfill Your promises.

CONTENTS

Introduction: How to Use This Book	i
The First Day *(Sunday)* Praise the LORD	1
The Second Day *(Monday)* Maturity in the Church	11
The Third Day *(Tuesday)* The Nations & The Day of the Lord	23
The Fourth Day: *(Wednesday)* Wisdom from Above	46
The Fifth Day: *(Thursday)* The Persecuted, Poor, & Oppressed	58
The Sixth Day: *(Friday)* Family & Friends, Neighbors & Enemies	73
The Seventh Day: *(Saturday)* Rest & Remember	88
Every Day: The Kingdom of God	98
Every Day: Blessings of the Righteous	109
Every Day: The Bride of Christ	112

Introduction
HOW TO USE THIS BOOK

God desires to reveal His Kingdom to us, bestow His richest blessings upon us as His people, and transform us into a Bride for His Son. It starts with prayer that is aligned with His will.

Too often, prayer is consumed with our own will, our own desires, and our own problems. No doubt, it is important to bring our needs, problems, and requests to God, and He desires for us to do so. But if this is the depth of our prayer life, it is very shallow.

True prayer is about aligning ourselves with God and His will. Through the Scriptures, God has revealed His will to us. For example, God has revealed:

- His desire for a holy people, a nation of God, composed of individuals who willingly offer themselves in His service to bring Him glory.
- His Sovereignty over all the nations of the earth and every global event, including the day of judgement to come.
- His wisdom and ways, sharing His secret counsels with those who fear Him.
- His love for those suffering for His name, and for the poor, the sojourner, the widow, the orphan, and the sick.
- His commandment to love one another as brothers and sisters in the household of God, and to love our neighbors and our enemies.
- His desire for us to enter into His rest as we trust in Him and remember all that He has done for us.
- How worthy He is of all praise, honor, adoration, and thanksgiving.

Deuteronomy 29:29 says, "The secret things belong to the LORD our God, but the things revealed belong to us and to our children forever, that we may follow all the words of this law." God has revealed His will to us so that we may *do it*. God's greatest desire is for our minds to be renewed to the likeness of His mind so that His will is done in the earth. Jesus told us to pray, "Your Kingdom come, Your will be done, on earth as it is in heaven." In heaven, everyone and everything is in total willing submission to God and His will. Accordingly, success in prayer is not about having our requests for our own needs met and answered. Success in prayer is when we have so aligned ourselves with God that His will is brought to pass in the earth without hindrance from our flesh, our own ideas, or the schemes of the evil one.

BACKGROUND OF DAILY PRAYER FOCUS

Years ago, the Lord asked me to live entirely by faith, not asking anyone for anything I need but simply trusting Him in prayer and obeying His voice. It was daunting and a shock to my system at first, as I was accustomed to being very self-willed and self-reliant. Letting go of control and my own way of doing things was challenging.

At that time, the Lord made it clear that if I kept my focus on the things that matter the most to Him, He would take care of the things that matter the most to me. (See Matthew 6:33; Joshua 1:8; Psalm 37:4; and Psalm 1.) To guide my times of prayer into His Word, His will, His truth, His purposes, and His heart, He gave me these Daily Prayer Focus categories. I have learned a tremendous amount about Him through this and He has been faithful to me - never failing to keep watch over all things pertaining to my life and well-being.

This book invites you to join me in praying through the Daily Prayer Focus topics that the Lord has given me. For each day's focus topic, an extensive but not all-inclusive list of Scriptures is given to help you begin to align your thoughts with God's will on the subject. Some of the Scripture passages provided for any given day may be longer than what you are accustomed to. But I encourage you to take your time to let the Word of God sink deep into your Spirit. Even if you only pray one passage of Scripture on a certain day with deepening understanding of and submission to God's Word and will, I believe this is better in God's sight than praying one thousand prayers out of self-will or trying to force God to bow to our desired outcomes and made up prophecies.

If you lack wisdom, ask God. He will give it to you. Ask Him to reveal His will to you, ask Him what He means, ask Him how things work... *ask, seek, knock* – not for your own desires but about His. Allow the Word of God to renew your mind. If what the Word says is different than your view of God, it is you who needs to change, not God.

Jesus will never fail you. When we abide in Him and He in us, we can ask whatever we wish and it will be done for us. (John 15:7.)

HOW TO USE THIS BOOK

The font of this book is large so that it is easy to read in prayer, even while kneeling before God with the book on the floor, standing, walking, or pacing as I often do in prayer times. God is not so concerned about our physical posture. But He is looking at the intent of our hearts as we approach Him. Let us do so with holy reverence.

Before you set out to pray according to these Daily Prayer Focus topics, I recommend clearing out your own cares and concerns. To do this, designate a separate time of prayer each day for your own needs or quickly cast your cares upon Jesus before opening to the Daily Prayer Focus Scriptures for the day. Once you have given your cares to Jesus, leave them in His very capable hands. If personal matters arise as you begin to pray the Daily Prayer Focus, have a piece of paper nearby to write it down so you will not be concerned about forgetting it later. Then, quickly resume in the Daily Prayer Focus. It can be very dangerous to mix your will with God's will or your anxieties with God's purposes, so try to avoid this as much as possible.

Turn to the Scriptures for whatever day of the week it is. If it is Monday, turn to Monday. If you miss a day or several days, just pick up and proceed to the day it is *today*. Whatever day(s) you missed will come around again next week, sure enough.

Here's how I use these Daily Prayer Focus Scriptures:
1. I open to the day's focus topic, scanning and reading through some of the Scriptures silently, inviting the Holy Spirit to guide me into the issues that God wants to highlight.

This is the priming the pump, so to speak.

2. Soon enough, the Holy Spirit causes one or two Scriptures, phrases, or sub-groups to "pop" off the page to me. I read them out loud. I will pause, meditate, repeat a Scripture, wait upon the Lord and continue reading until I sense the Holy Spirit stirring within me to move me into prayer. This is like pumping the pump until the water comes.

3. Once the Holy Spirit is stirred within me and ready to pour out, I pray according to whatever the Lord reveals to my heart and speak forth the word that the Lord puts into my mouth. When we do not know how to pray as we ought, the Holy Spirit knows. Praying and speaking out what the Holy Spirit gives is the rivers of living water Jesus promised would pour out of our inmost being. Praise the Lord for His faithfulness!

If the Lord shows you another way to use this book, do whatever He says. Simply having so many Scriptures compiled on these subjects may stir you to deeper reflection, study, and meditation on the Word and ways of God.

In whatever way you use this book, I pray it is a blessing to you. May the Lord release to you the spirit of wisdom and revelation as you grow in your knowledge of Him and as you learn to pray prayers in alignment with His will and purposes.

By His grace,
Wendy Bowen

2022 UPDATED EDITION

This 2022 Edition has been updated with Chapter Indexes of Topics on each day. The days of the week also begin with the first day, Sunday, and end with Saturday, the seventh day, the Sabbath rest of God, in accordance with the Biblical pattern on the days of the week.

Lastly, the cover of the book has been redesigned as one of Manifest International's Core Curriculum books. Although it is not a course for studying, the training for this is in the *doing* of it. Forsaking our own will to align ourselves with God's will is truly at the core of the way we approach prayer.

Be blessed!

The First Day (Sunday)
PRAISE THE LORD

INDEX OF TOPICS:
- Heaven's Praise
- Psalms of Praise List
- Praise Scriptures
- Thanksgiving & Thankfulness for what God has Done
- New Testament Praise
- Songs of Praise & Deliverance

HEAVEN'S PRAISE

Revelation 5:9: And they sang a new song, saying: "**You are worthy** to take the scroll and to open its seals, because you were slain, and with your blood you purchased for God persons from every tribe and language and people and nation.

Revelation 5:12: In a loud voice they were saying: "**Worthy is the Lamb**, who was slain, to receive power and wealth and wisdom and strength and **honor and glory and praise!**"

Revelation 5:13-14: Then I heard every creature in heaven and on earth and under the earth and on the sea, and all that is in them, saying: "**To him who sits on the throne and to the Lamb be praise and honor and glory** and power, for ever and ever!" The four living creatures said, "Amen," and the elders fell down and worshiped.

Revelation 7:11-12: All the angels were standing around the throne and around the elders and the four living creatures. They fell down on their faces before the throne and worshiped God, saying: "Amen! **Praise and glory** and wisdom and thanks and honor and power and strength be to our God for ever and ever. Amen!"

Revelation 11:16-18: And the twenty-four elders, who were seated on their thrones before God, fell on their faces and **worshiped God**, saying: "**We give thanks to you, Lord God Almighty**, the One who is and who was, because you have taken your great power and have begun to reign. The nations were angry, and your wrath has come. The time has come for judging the dead, and for rewarding your servants the prophets and your people who revere your name, both great and small – and for destroying those who destroy the earth."

Revelation 14:6-7: Then I saw another angel flying in midair, and he had the eternal gospel to proclaim to those who live on the earth – to every nation, tribe, language and people.

He said in a loud voice, "Fear God and **give him glory**, because the hour of his judgment has come. **Worship him** who made the heavens, the earth, the sea and the springs of water."

Revelation 15:2-4: And I saw what looked like a sea of glass glowing with fire and, standing beside the sea, those who had been victorious over the beast and its image and over the number of its name. They held harps given them by God and sang the song of God's servant Moses and of the Lamb: "**Great and marvelous are your deeds, Lord God Almighty. Just and true are your ways, King of the nations.** Who will not fear you, Lord, and **bring glory to your name**? For you alone are holy. All nations will come and worship before you, for your righteous acts have been revealed."

Revelation 19:1-8: After this I heard what sounded like the roar of a great multitude in heaven shouting: "**Hallelujah! Salvation and glory and power belong to our God, for true and just are his judgments**. He has condemned the great prostitute who corrupted the earth by her adulteries. He has avenged on her the blood of his servants." And again they shouted: "**Hallelujah!** The smoke from her [Babylon] goes up for ever and ever." The twenty-four elders and the four living creatures fell down and worshiped God, who was seated on the throne. And they cried: "**Amen, Hallelujah!**" Then a voice came from the throne, saying: "**Praise our God, all you his servants, you who fear him, both great and small!**" Then I heard what sounded like a great multitude, like the roar of rushing waters and like loud peals of thunder, shouting: "**Hallelujah! For our Lord God Almighty reigns. Let us rejoice and be glad and give him glory!** For the wedding of the Lamb has come, and his bride has made herself ready. Fine linen, bright and clean, was given her to wear." (Fine linen stands for the righteous acts of God's holy people.)

PSALMS OF PRAISE

Psalm 8	Psalm 65	Psalm 89	Psalm 113
Psalm 18	Psalm 66	Psalm 97	Psalm 134
Psalm 29	Psalm 67	Psalm 103	Psalm 135
Psalm 30	Psalm 68	Psalm 104	Psalm 136
Psalm 47	Psalm 84	Psalm 111	Psalm 145

Psalm 117:1-2: **Praise the LORD**, all you nations; extol him, all you peoples. For great is his love toward us, and the faithfulness of the LORD endures forever. **Praise the LORD**.

Psalm 100:1-5: **A psalm. For giving grateful praise.** Shout for joy to the LORD, all the earth. **Worship the LORD** with gladness; come before him with joyful songs. Know that the LORD is God. It is he who made us, and we are his; we are his people, the sheep of his pasture. **Enter his gates with thanksgiving and his courts with praise; give thanks to him and praise his name.** For the LORD is good and his love endures forever; his faithfulness continues through all generations.

Psalm 134:1-2: **Praise the LORD**, all you servants of the LORD who minister by night in the house of the LORD. Lift up your hands in the sanctuary and **praise the LORD.**

Psalm 67:1-7: May God be gracious to us and bless us and make his face shine on us – so that your ways may be known on earth, your salvation among all nations. **May the peoples praise you, God; may all the peoples praise you.** May the nations be glad and sing for joy, for you rule the peoples with equity and guide the nations of the earth. **May the peoples praise you, God; may all the peoples praise you.** The land yields its harvest; God, our God, blesses us. May God bless us still, so that all the ends of the earth will fear him.

Psalm 96:1-13: Sing to the LORD a new song; sing to the LORD, all the earth. Sing to the LORD, **praise his name**; proclaim his salvation day after day. **Declare his glory** among the nations, his marvelous deeds among all peoples. For great is the LORD and most worthy of praise; he is to be feared above all gods. For all the gods of the nations are idols, but the LORD made the heavens. Splendor and majesty are before him; strength and glory are in his sanctuary. **Ascribe to the LORD**, all you families of nations, **ascribe to the LORD glory and strength. Ascribe to the LORD the glory due his name**; bring an offering and come into his courts. **Worship the LORD in the splendor of his holiness**; tremble before him, all the earth. Say among the nations, "The LORD reigns." The world is firmly established, it cannot be moved; he will judge the peoples with equity. **Let the heavens rejoice, let the earth be glad**; let the sea resound, and all that is in it. Let the fields be jubilant, and everything in them; let all the trees of the forest sing for joy. **Let all creation rejoice before the LORD**, for he comes, he comes to judge the earth. He will judge the world in righteousness and the peoples in his faithfulness.

Psalm 111:1-10: **Praise the LORD.** I will extol the LORD with all my heart in the council of the upright and in the assembly. Great are the works of the LORD; they are pondered by all who delight in them. Glorious and majestic are his deeds, and his righteousness endures forever. He has caused his wonders to be remembered; the LORD is gracious and compassionate. He provides food for those who fear him; he remembers his covenant forever. He has shown his people the power of his works, giving them the lands of other nations. The works of his hands are faithful and just; all his precepts are trustworthy. They are established for ever and ever, enacted in faithfulness and uprightness. He provided redemption for his people; he ordained his covenant forever – holy and awesome is his name. The fear of the LORD is the beginning of wisdom; all who follow his precepts have good understanding. **To him belongs eternal praise.**

Psalm 148:1-14: **Praise the LORD. Praise the LORD from the heavens; praise him in the heights above. Praise him, all his angels; praise him, all his heavenly hosts. Praise him, sun and moon; praise him, all you shining stars. Praise him, you highest heavens and you waters above the skies. Let them praise the name of the LORD**, for at his command they were created, and he established them for ever and ever – he issued a decree that will never pass away. Praise the LORD from the earth, you great sea creatures and all ocean depths, lightning and hail, snow and clouds, stormy winds that do his bidding, you mountains and all hills, fruit trees and all cedars, wild animals and all cattle, small creatures and flying birds, kings of the earth and all nations, you princes and all rulers on earth, young men and women, old men and children. Let them praise the name of the LORD, for his

The First Day (Sunday): Praise

name alone is exalted; his splendor is above the earth and the heavens. And he has raised up for his people a horn, the praise of all his faithful servants, of Israel, the people close to his heart. Praise the LORD.

Psalm 149:1-9: **Praise the LORD.** Sing to the LORD a new song, **his praise** in the assembly of his faithful people. Let Israel rejoice in their Maker; let the people of Zion be glad in their King. Let them **praise his name with dancing and make music to him with timbrel and harp.** For the LORD takes delight in his people; he crowns the humble with victory. Let his faithful people rejoice in this honor and sing for joy on their beds. **May the praise of God be in their mouths** and a double-edged sword in their hands, to inflict vengeance on the nations and punishment on the peoples, to bind their kings with fetters, their nobles with shackles of iron, to carry out the sentence written against them – this is the glory of all his faithful people. **Praise the LORD.**

Psalm 150:1-6: **Praise the LORD. Praise God** in his sanctuary; **praise him** in his mighty heavens. **Praise him** for his acts of power; praise him for his surpassing greatness. **Praise him** with the sounding of the trumpet, **praise him** with the harp and lyre, **praise him** with timbrel and dancing, **praise him** with the strings and pipe, **praise him** with the clash of cymbals, **praise him** with resounding cymbals. **Let everything that has breath praise the LORD. Praise the LORD.**

PRAISE SCRIPTURES

Psalm 59:16-17: But I will sing of your strength, in the morning I will sing of your love; for you are my fortress, my refuge in times of trouble. You are my strength, **I sing praise to you**; you, God, are my fortress, my God on whom I can rely.

Psalm 69:30-31: **I will praise God's name in song and glorify him with thanksgiving.** This will please the LORD more than an ox, more than a bull with its horns and hooves.

2 Chronicles 20:21-22: After consulting the people, Jehoshaphat appointed men to sing to the LORD and to **praise him for the splendor of his holiness** as they went out at the head of the army, saying: "**Give thanks to the LORD, for his love endures forever.**" As they began to **sing and praise**, the LORD set ambushes against the men of Ammon and Moab and Mount Seir who were invading Judah, and they were defeated.

Psalm 16:7: I will **praise the LORD**, who counsels me; even at night my heart instructs me.

Psalm 21:13: **Be exalted** in your strength, LORD; we will sing and **praise your might.**

Psalm 40:3: He put a new song in my mouth, **a hymn of praise to our God.** Many will see and fear the LORD and put their trust in him.

Psalm 41:13: **Praise be to the LORD**, the God of Israel, from everlasting to everlasting. Amen and Amen.

Psalm 44:8: In God we make our boast all day long, and **we will praise your name forever**.

1 Chronicles 29:10-13: **David praised the LORD** in the presence of the whole assembly, saying, "**Praise be to you, LORD**, the God of our father Israel, from everlasting to everlasting. **Yours, LORD, is the greatness and the power and the glory and the majesty and the splendor**, for everything in heaven and earth is yours. **Yours, LORD, is the kingdom; you are exalted as head over all**. Wealth and honor come from you; you are the ruler of all things. In your hands are strength and power to exalt and give strength to all. **Now, our God, we give you thanks, and praise your glorious name**.

2 Chronicles 5:12-14: All the Levites who were musicians – Asaph, Heman, Jeduthun and their sons and relatives – stood on the east side of the altar, dressed in fine linen and playing cymbals, harps and lyres. They were accompanied by 120 priests sounding trumpets. **The trumpeters and musicians joined in unison to give praise and thanks to the LORD**. Accompanied by trumpets, cymbals and other instruments, **the singers raised their voices in praise to the LORD and sang: "He is good; his love endures forever."** Then the temple of the LORD was filled with the cloud, and the priests could not perform their service because of the cloud, for the glory of the LORD filled the temple of God.

Psalm 72:18-19: **Praise be to the LORD God**, the God of Israel, who alone does marvelous deeds. **Praise be to his glorious name forever**; may the whole earth be filled with his glory. Amen and Amen.

Nehemiah 9:5-6: And the Levites... said: "**Stand up and praise the LORD your God**, who is from everlasting to everlasting." "Blessed be your glorious name, and may it be exalted above all blessing and praise. You alone are the LORD. You made the heavens, even the highest heavens, and all their starry host, the earth and all that is on it, the seas and all that is in them. You give life to everything, and the multitudes of heaven worship you.

Deuteronomy 32:3: I will proclaim the name of the LORD. **Oh, praise the greatness of our God!**

Psalm 71:6, 8, 14-17, 22-24: From birth I have relied on you; you brought me forth from my mother's womb. **I will ever praise you. ... My mouth is filled with your praise**, declaring your splendor all day long. ... As for me, I will always have hope; **I will praise you more and more**. My mouth will tell of your righteous deeds, of your saving acts all day long – though I know not how to relate them all. I will come and proclaim your mighty acts, Sovereign LORD; I will proclaim your righteous deeds, yours alone. Since my youth, God, you have taught me, and to this day I declare your marvelous deeds. ... **I will praise you with the harp for your faithfulness, my God; I will sing praise to you with the lyre, Holy One of Israel. My lips will shout for joy when I sing praise to you** – I whom you have delivered. My tongue will tell of your righteous acts all day long, for those who wanted to harm me have been put to shame and confusion.

Psalm 75:1: **We praise you, God, we praise you**, for your Name is near; people tell of your wonderful deeds.

The First Day (Sunday): Praise

Psalm 105:1-4: **Give praise to the LORD**, proclaim his name; make known among the nations what he has done. **Sing to him, sing praise to him**; tell of all his wonderful acts. **Glory in his holy name**; let the hearts of those who seek the LORD rejoice. Look to the LORD and his strength; seek his face always.

Psalm 118:28: You are my God, and **I will praise you; you are my God, and I will exalt you**.

Psalm 119:7, 12, 108, 164, 171, 175: **I will praise you** with an upright heart as I learn your righteous laws. ... Praise be to you, LORD; teach me your decrees. ... **Accept, LORD, the willing praise of my mouth**, and teach me your laws. ... **Seven times a day I praise you** for your righteous laws. ... **May my lips overflow with praise**, for you teach me your decrees. ... **Let me live that I may praise you**, and may your laws sustain me.

Psalm 138:1-2: **I will praise you, LORD, with all my heart; before the "gods" I will sing your praise**. I will bow down toward your holy temple and will **praise your name** for your unfailing love and your faithfulness, for you have so exalted your solemn decree that it surpasses your fame.

Psalm 146:1-2: **Praise the LORD. Praise the LORD, my soul.** I will **praise the LORD** all my life; I will **sing praise to my God as long as I live**.

Isaiah 25:1-9: **LORD, you are my God; I will exalt you and praise your name**, for in perfect faithfulness you have done wonderful things, things planned long ago. You have made the city a heap of rubble, the fortified town a ruin, the foreigners' stronghold a city no more; it will never be rebuilt. Therefore strong peoples will honor you; cities of ruthless nations will revere you. You have been a refuge for the poor, a refuge for the needy in their distress, a shelter from the storm and a shade from the heat. For the breath of the ruthless is like a storm driving against a wall and like the heat of the desert. You silence the uproar of foreigners; as heat is reduced by the shadow of a cloud, so the song of the ruthless is stilled. On this mountain the LORD Almighty will prepare a feast of rich food for all peoples, a banquet of aged wine – the best of meats and the finest of wines. On this mountain he will destroy the shroud that enfolds all peoples, the sheet that covers all nations; he will swallow up death forever. The Sovereign LORD will wipe away the tears from all faces; he will remove his people's disgrace from all the earth. The LORD has spoken. In that day they will say, "Surely this is our God; we trusted in him, and he saved us. This is the LORD, we trusted in him; **let us rejoice and be glad in his salvation**."

PRAISE AS THANKSGIVING & THANKFULNESS FOR WHAT GOD HAS DONE

Psalm 13:6: I will **sing the LORD's praise**, for he has been good to me.

Psalm 52:9: For what you have done **I will always praise you** in the presence of your faithful people. And I will hope in your name, for your name is good.

Psalm 28:6-7: **Praise be to the LORD**, for he has heard my cry for mercy. The LORD is my strength and my shield; my heart trusts in him, and he helps me. My heart leaps for joy, and **with my song I praise him.**

Psalm 54:6-7: I will sacrifice a freewill offering to you; **I will praise your name, LORD,** for it is good. You have delivered me from all my troubles, and my eyes have looked in triumph on my foes.

Psalm 56:10-13: **In God, whose word I praise, in the LORD, whose word I praise** – in God I trust and am not afraid. What can man do to me? I am under vows to you, my God; **I will present my thank offerings to you.** For you have delivered me from death and my feet from stumbling, that I may walk before God in the light of life.

Psalm 63:2-7: I have seen you in the sanctuary and beheld your power and your glory. **Because your love is better than life, my lips will glorify you. I will praise you as long as I live, and in your name I will lift up my hands.** I will be fully satisfied as with the richest of foods; with singing lips my mouth will praise you. On my bed I remember you; I think of you through the watches of the night. Because you are my help, I sing in the shadow of your wings.

Psalm 86:12-13: **I will praise you, Lord my God, with all my heart; I will glorify your name forever.** For great is your love toward me; you have delivered me from the depths, from the realm of the dead.

Psalm 139:14: **I praise you** because I am fearfully and wonderfully made; your works are wonderful, I know that full well.

Psalm 144:1: **Praise be to the LORD** my Rock, who trains my hands for war, my fingers for battle.

Deuteronomy 8:10: When you have eaten and are satisfied, **praise the LORD your God** for the good land he has given you.

1 Kings 8:56: "**Praise be to the LORD**, who has given rest to his people Israel just as he promised. Not one word has failed of all the good promises he gave through his servant Moses.

1 Kings 10:9: **Praise be to the LORD your God**, who has delighted in you and placed you on the throne of Israel. Because of the LORD's eternal love for Israel, he has made you king to maintain justice and righteousness."

NEW TESTAMENT PRAISE & THANKSGIVING

1 Peter 2:9: But you are a chosen people, a royal priesthood, a holy nation, God's special possession, **that you may declare the praises** of him who called you out of darkness into his wonderful light.

The First Day (Sunday): Praise

Hebrews 13:15: Through Jesus, therefore, **let us continually offer to God a sacrifice of praise** – the fruit of lips that openly profess his name.

Matthew 11:25-26: At that time Jesus said, "**I praise you, Father, Lord of heaven and earth**, because you have hidden these things from the wise and learned, and revealed them to little children. Yes, Father, for this is what you were pleased to do. (See also Luke 10:21.)

Luke 5:26: Everyone was amazed and **gave praise to God**. They were filled with awe and said, "We have seen remarkable things today."

Luke 19:37: When he came near the place where the road goes down the Mount of Olives, the whole **crowd of disciples began joyfully to praise God in loud voices for all the miracles they had seen**:

Luke 17:18: Has no one returned to **give praise to God** except this foreigner?"

2 Corinthians 1:3-4: **Praise be to the God and Father of our Lord Jesus Christ**, the Father of compassion and the God of all comfort, who comforts us in all our troubles, so that we can comfort those in any trouble with the comfort we ourselves receive from God.

Ephesians 1:3-6: **Praise be to the God and Father of our Lord Jesus Christ**, who has blessed us in the heavenly realms with every spiritual blessing in Christ. For he chose us in him before the creation of the world to be holy and blameless in his sight. In love he predestined us for adoption to sonship through Jesus Christ, in accordance with his pleasure and will – **to the praise of his glorious grace, which he has freely given us in the One he loves**.

1 Peter 1:3-5: **Praise be to the God and Father of our Lord Jesus Christ!** In his great mercy he has given us new birth into a living hope through the resurrection of Jesus Christ from the dead, and into an inheritance that can never perish, spoil or fade. This inheritance is kept in heaven for you, who through faith are shielded by God's power until the coming of the salvation that is ready to be revealed in the last time.

1 Peter 4:16: However, if you suffer as a Christian, do not be ashamed, but **praise God that you bear that name**.

Acts 12:23: Immediately, because Herod **did not give praise to God**, an angel of the Lord struck him down, and he was eaten by worms and died.

Colossians 3:17: And whatever you do, whether in word or deed, do it all in the name of the Lord Jesus, **giving thanks to God the Father through him.**

Ephesians 5:18-20: Do not get drunk on wine, which leads to debauchery. Instead, be filled with the Spirit, speaking to one another with psalms, hymns, and songs from the Spirit. Sing and make music from your heart to the Lord, **always giving thanks to God the Father for everything**, in the name of our Lord Jesus Christ.

Colossians 2:7: rooted and built up in him, strengthened in the faith as you were taught, and **overflowing with thankfulness**.

1 Thessalonians 5:18: **give thanks in all circumstances**; for this is God's will for you in Christ Jesus.

Ephesians 5:4: Nor should there be obscenity, foolish talk or coarse joking, which are out of place, **but rather thanksgiving**.

SONGS OF PRAISE & DELIVERANCE

The Song of Moses:
Exodus 15:1-19: Then Moses and the Israelites sang this song to the LORD: "I will sing to the LORD, for he is highly exalted. Both horse and driver he has hurled into the sea. "The LORD is my strength and my defense; he has become my salvation. He is my God, and I will praise him, my father's God, and I will exalt him. The LORD is a warrior; the LORD is his name. Pharaoh's chariots and his army he has hurled into the sea. The best of Pharaoh's officers are drowned in the Red Sea. The deep waters have covered them; they sank to the depths like a stone. Your right hand, LORD, was majestic in power. Your right hand, LORD, shattered the enemy. "In the greatness of your majesty you threw down those who opposed you. You unleashed your burning anger; it consumed them like stubble. By the blast of your nostrils the waters piled up. The surging waters stood up like a wall; the deep waters congealed in the heart of the sea. The enemy boasted, 'I will pursue, I will overtake them. I will divide the spoils; I will gorge myself on them. I will draw my sword and my hand will destroy them.' But you blew with your breath, and the sea covered them. They sank like lead in the mighty waters. Who among the gods is like you, LORD? Who is like you--majestic in holiness, awesome in glory, working wonders? "You stretch out your right hand, and the earth swallows your enemies. In your unfailing love you will lead the people you have redeemed. In your strength you will guide them to your holy dwelling. The nations will hear and tremble; anguish will grip the people of Philistia. The chiefs of Edom will be terrified, the leaders of Moab will be seized with trembling, the people of Canaan will melt away; terror and dread will fall on them. By the power of your arm they will be as still as a stone--until your people pass by, LORD, until the people you bought pass by. You will bring them in and plant them on the mountain of your inheritance--the place, LORD, you made for your dwelling, the sanctuary, Lord, your hands established. "The LORD reigns for ever and ever." When Pharaoh's horses, chariots and horsemen went into the sea, the LORD brought the waters of the sea back over them, but the Israelites walked through the sea on dry ground.

Mary's Song:
Luke 1:46-55: And Mary said: "My soul glorifies the Lord and my spirit rejoices in God my Savior, for he has been mindful of the humble state of his servant. From now on all generations will call me blessed, for the Mighty One has done great things for me – holy is his name. His mercy extends to those who fear him, from generation to generation. He has performed mighty deeds with his arm; he has scattered those who are proud in their

inmost thoughts. He has brought down rulers from their thrones but has lifted up the humble. He has filled the hungry with good things but has sent the rich away empty. He has helped his servant Israel, remembering to be merciful to Abraham and his descendants forever, just as he promised our ancestors."

Zechariah's Song:
Luke 1:68-79: "Praise be to the Lord, the God of Israel, because he has come to his people and redeemed them. He has raised up a horn of salvation for us in the house of his servant David (as he said through his holy prophets of long ago), salvation from our enemies and from the hand of all who hate us – to show mercy to our ancestors and to remember his holy covenant, the oath he swore to our father Abraham: to rescue us from the hand of our enemies, and to enable us to serve him without fear in holiness and righteousness before him all our days. And you, my child, will be called a prophet of the Most High; for you will go on before the Lord to prepare the way for him, to give his people the knowledge of salvation through the forgiveness of their sins, because of the tender mercy of our God, by which the rising sun will come to us from heaven to shine on those living in darkness and in the shadow of death, to guide our feet into the path of peace."

See Also:

Deborah's Song:	*David's Song:*	*Confession Song:*	*Song for Mercy:*
Judges 5:1-31	2 Samuel 22	Nehemiah 9:5-38	Habakkuk 3

The Second Day (Monday)
MATURITY IN THE CHURCH

INDEX OF TOPICS:
- Paul's Prayers for the Church
- Maturity Scriptures
- Love One Another - the Greatest of These Is Love
- Revelation Churches Exhorted to Maturity
- Maturity for Church Leadership
- Unity Scriptures
- Jesus' Prayer for Disciples - the High Priestly Prayer

PAUL'S PRAYERS FOR THE CHURCH

Colossians 1:9-14: For this reason, since the day we heard about you, we have not stopped praying for you. We continually ask God to fill you with the knowledge of his will through all the wisdom and understanding that the Spirit gives, so that you may live a life worthy of the Lord and please him in every way: bearing fruit in every good work, growing in the knowledge of God, being strengthened with all power according to his glorious might so that you may have great endurance and patience, and giving joyful thanks to the Father, who has qualified you to share in the inheritance of his holy people in the kingdom of light. For he has rescued us from the dominion of darkness and brought us into the kingdom of the Son he loves, in whom we have redemption, the forgiveness of sins.

Philippians 1:9-11: And this is my prayer: that your love may abound more and more in knowledge and depth of insight, so that you may be able to discern what is best and may be pure and blameless for the day of Christ, filled with the fruit of righteousness that comes through Jesus Christ – to the glory and praise of God.

Ephesians 1:15-23: For this reason, ever since I heard about your faith in the Lord Jesus and your love for all God's people, I have not stopped giving thanks for you, remembering you in my prayers. I keep asking that the God of our Lord Jesus Christ, the glorious Father, may give you the Spirit of wisdom and revelation, so that you may know him better. I pray that the eyes of your heart may be enlightened in order that you may know the hope to which he has called you, the riches of his glorious inheritance in his holy people, and his incomparably great power for us who believe. That power is the same as the mighty strength he exerted when he raised Christ from the dead and seated him at his right hand in the heavenly realms, far above all rule and authority, power and dominion, and every name that is invoked, not only in the present age but also in the one to come. And God placed all things under his feet and appointed him to be head over everything for the church, which is his body, the fullness of him who fills everything in every way.

Ephesians 3:14-20: For this reason I kneel before the Father, from whom every family in heaven and on earth derives its name. I pray that out of his glorious riches he may strengthen you with power through his Spirit in your inner being, so that Christ may dwell in your hearts through faith. And I pray that you, being rooted and established in love, may have power, together with all the Lord's holy people, to grasp how wide and long and high and deep is the love of Christ, and to know this love that surpasses knowledge – that you may be filled to the measure of all the fullness of God. Now to him who is able to do immeasurably more than all we ask or imagine, according to his power that is at work within us,

1 Thessalonians 3:12-13: May the Lord make your love increase and overflow for each other and for everyone else, just as ours does for you. May he strengthen your hearts so that you will be blameless and holy in the presence of our God and Father when our Lord Jesus comes with all his holy ones.

2 Thessalonians 1:11-12: With this in mind, we constantly pray for you, that our God may make you worthy of his calling, and that by his power he may bring to fruition your every desire for goodness and your every deed prompted by faith. We pray this so that the name of our Lord Jesus may be glorified in you, and you in him, according to the grace of our God and the Lord Jesus Christ.

MATURITY SCRIPTURES

Ephesians 4:11-16: So Christ himself gave the apostles, the prophets, the evangelists, the pastors and teachers, to equip his people for works of service, so that the body of Christ may be built up until we all reach unity in the faith and in the knowledge of the Son of God and **become mature**, attaining to the **whole measure of the fullness of Christ**. Then we will **no longer be infants**, tossed back and forth by the waves, and blown here and there by every wind of teaching and by the cunning and craftiness of people in their deceitful scheming. Instead, speaking the truth in love, we will **grow to become in every respect the mature body** of him who is the head, that is, Christ. From him the whole body, joined and held together by every supporting ligament, grows and builds itself up in love, as each part does its work.

Hebrews 5:11-6:2: It is hard to make it clear to you because you no longer try to understand. In fact, though by this time you ought to be teachers, you need someone to teach you the elementary truths of God's Word all over again. You need milk, not solid food! Anyone who lives on milk, being still an infant, is not acquainted with the teaching about righteousness. But **solid food is for the mature**, who by constant use have trained themselves to distinguish between good and evil. Therefore let us move beyond the elementary teachings about Christ and be **taken forward to maturity**, not laying again the foundation of repentance from acts that lead to death, and of faith in God, instruction about cleansing rites, the laying on of hands, the resurrection of the dead, and eternal judgment. And God permitting, we will do so.

Hebrews 6:11-12: We want each of you to show this same diligence to the very end, so that what you hope for may be fully realized. We do not want you to become lazy, but imitate those who through faith and patience inherit what has been promised.

Matthew 5:43-48: You have heard that it was said, "Love your neighbor and hate your enemy." But I tell you, love your enemies and pray for those who persecute you, that you may be children of your Father in Heaven. He causes His sun to rise on the evil and the good, and sends rain on the righteous and the unrighteous. If you love those who love you, what reward will you get? Are not even the tax collectors doing that? And if you greet only your own people, what are you doing more than others? Do not even pagans do that? **Be perfect [mature],** therefore, as your heavenly Father is **perfect [mature.]**

Colossians 4:12: Epaphras, who is one of you and a servant of Christ Jesus, sends greetings. He is always wrestling in prayer for you, that you may stand firm in all the will of God, **mature** and fully assured.

Philippians 3:7-16: But whatever were gains to me I now consider loss for the sake of Christ. What is more, I consider everything a loss because of the surpassing worth of knowing Christ Jesus my Lord, for whose sake I have lost all things. I consider them garbage that I may gain Christ and be found in Him, not having a righteousness of my own that comes from the law, but that which is through faith in Christ – the righteousness that comes from God on the basis of faith. I want to know Christ – yes, to know the power of His resurrection and participation in His sufferings, becoming like Him in His death, and so, somehow, attaining to the resurrection from the dead.
Not that I have already obtained all this, or have already arrived at my goal, but I press on to take hold of that for which Christ Jesus took hold of me. Brothers and sisters, I do not consider myself yet to have taken hold of it. But one thing I do: Forgetting what is behind and straining toward what is ahead, I press on toward the goal to win the prize for which God has called me heavenward in Christ Jesus. **All of us, then, who are mature should take such a view of things**. And if on some point you think differently, that too God will make clear to you. Only let us live up to what we have already attained.

Matthew 19:21: Jesus answered, "If you want to be **perfect [mature]**, go, sell your possessions and give to the poor, and you will have treasure in heaven. Then come, follow me."

2 Peter 1:3-4: His divine power has given us everything we need for a godly life through our knowledge of Him who called us by His own glory and goodness. Through these He has given us His very great and precious promises, so that through them you may participate in the divine nature, having escaped the corruption in the world caused by evil desires.

The Second Day (Monday): Maturity in the Church

1 Corinthians 2:6-16: We do, however, speak a message of wisdom **among the mature**, but not the wisdom of this age or of the rulers of this age, who are coming to nothing. No, we declare God's wisdom, a mystery that has been hidden and that God destined for our glory before time began. None of the rulers of this age understood it, for if they had, they would not have crucified the Lord of glory. However, as it is written, what no eye has seen, what no ear has heard, and what no human mind has conceived, the things God has prepared for those who love Him (quoting Isaiah 64:4) these are the things God has revealed to us by His Spirit. The Spirit searches all things, even the deep things of God. For who knows a person's thought except their own spirit within them? In the same way no one knows the thought of God except the Spirit of God. What we have receive is not the spirit of the world, but the Spirit who is from God, so that we may understand what God has freely given us. This is what we speak, not in words taught by human wisdom but in words taught by the Spirit, explaining Spiritual realities with Spirit-taught words. The person without the Spirit does not accept the things that come from the Spirit of God but considers them foolishness, and cannot understand them because they are discerned only through the Spirit. The person with the Spirit makes judgments about all things, but such a person is not subject to merely human judgments, for "Who has known the mind of the Lord so as to instruct Him?" (Quoting Isaiah 40:13) **But we have the mind of Christ**.

1 Corinthians 14:20: Brothers and sisters, stop thinking like children. In regard to evil be infants, but in your thinking **be adults [mature]**.

James 1:2-4: Consider it pure joy, my brothers and sisters, whenever you face trials of many kinds, because you know that the testing of your faith produces perseverance. Let perseverance finish its work so **that you may be mature and complete**, not lacking anything.

2 Peter 1:5-11: For this reason, **make every effort to add to your faith**, goodness; and to goodness, knowledge; and to knowledge, self-control; and to self-control, perseverance; and to perseverance, godliness; and to godliness, brotherly affection; and to brotherly affection, love. For if you possess these qualities in increasing measure, they will **keep you from being ineffective and unproductive** in your knowledge of our Lord Jesus Christ. But whoever does not have them is nearsighted and blind, forgetting that they have been cleansed from their past sins. Therefore, my brothers and sisters, make every effort to confirm that you are among those who God has called and chosen. For if you do these things, you will never stumble, and you will receive a rich welcome into the eternal Kingdom of our Lord and Savior Jesus Christ.

Colossians 1:24-28: Now I rejoice in what I am suffering for you, and I fill up in my flesh what is still lacking in regard to Christ's afflictions, for the sake of His Body, which is the Church. I have become its servant by the commission God gave me to present to you the Word of God in its fullness – the mystery that has been kept hidden for ages and generations, but is now disclosed to the Lord's people. To them God has chosen to make known among the Gentiles the glorious riches of this mystery, which is Christ in you, the hope of glory. He is the one we proclaim, admonishing and teaching everyone with all wisdom, so that we may **present everyone fully mature in Christ**. To this end I strenuously contend with all the energy Christ so powerfully works in me.

Romans 6:3-14: All of us who were baptized into Christ Jesus were baptized into His death! We were therefore buried with Him through baptism into death in order that, just as Christ was raised from the dead through the glory of the Father, we too may live a new life. For if we have been united with Him in a death like His, we will certainly also be united with Him in a resurrection like His. For we know that our old self was crucified with Him so that the body ruled by sin might be done away with, that we should no longer be slaves to sin – because anyone who has died has been set free from sin. Now if we died with Christ, we believe that we will also live with Him. For we know that since Christ was raised from the dead, He cannot die again – death no longer has mastery over Him. The death He died, He died to sin once for all – but the life He lives, He lives to God. In the same way, count yourselves dead to sin but alive to God in Christ Jesus. Therefore do not let sin reign in your mortal body so that you obey its evil desires. Do not offer any part of yourself to sin as an instrument of wickedness, but rather **offer yourselves to God as those who have been brought from death to life; and offer every part of yourself to Him as an instrument of righteousness**. For sin shall no longer be your master, because you are not under law, but under grace.

James 3:1-2: [Maturity shown by control of the tongue] Not many of you should become teachers, my fellow believers, because you know that we who teach will be judged more strictly. We all stumble in many ways. Anyone who is never at fault in what they say is **perfect [mature], able to keep their whole body in check**.

1 Peter 1:14-15: As obedient children, do not conform to the evil desires you had when you lived in ignorance. But just as He who called you is holy, so be holy in all you do; for it is written, "Be holy, because I am holy." (Quoting Leviticus 11:44, 19:2.)

LOVE ONE ANOTHER - THE GREATEST OF THESE IS LOVE

John 13:34-35: A new command I give you: **Love one another. As I have loved you, so you must love one another.** By this everyone will know that you are my disciples, if you **love one another.**

John 15:12-17: [Love One Another] My command is this: **Love each other as I have loved you. Greater love has no one than this: to lay down one's life for one's friends.** You are my friends if you do what I command. I no longer call you servants, because a servant does not know his master's business. Instead, I have called you friends, for everything that I learned from my Father I have made known to you. You did not choose me, but I chose you and appointed you so that you might go and bear fruit – fruit that will last – and so that whatever you ask in my name the Father will give you. This is my command: **Love each other.**

1 Corinthians 13:1-4: If I speak in the tongues of men or of angels, but do not have **love**, I

am only a resounding gong or a clanging cymbal. If I have the gift of prophecy and can fathom all mysteries and all knowledge, and if I have a faith that can move mountains, but do not have **love**, I am nothing. If I give all I possess to the poor and give over my body to hardship that I may boast, but do not have **love**, I gain nothing.

1 Corinthians 13:4-13: **Love** is patient, love is kind. **It** does not envy, **it** does not boast, **it** is not proud. **It** does not dishonor others, **it** is not self-seeking, **it** is not easily angered, **it** keeps no record of wrongs. **Love** does not delight in evil but rejoices with the truth. **It** always protects, always trusts, always hopes, always perseveres. **Love** never fails. But where there are prophecies, they will cease; where there are tongues, they will be stilled; where there is knowledge, it will pass away. For we know in part and we prophesy in part, but when completeness comes, what is in part disappears. When I was a child, I talked like a child, I thought like a child, I reasoned like a child. When I became a man, I put the ways of childhood behind me. For now we see only a reflection as in a mirror; then we shall see face to face. Now I know in part; then I shall know fully, even as I am fully known. And now these three remain: faith, hope and **love. But the greatest of these is love**.

Romans 12:9-18: **Love must be sincere**. Hate what is evil; cling to what is good. Be devoted to one another in love. Honor one another above yourselves. Never be lacking in zeal, but keep your spiritual fervor, serving the Lord. Be joyful in hope, patient in affliction, faithful in prayer. Share with the Lord's people who are in need. Practice hospitality. Bless those who persecute you; bless and do not curse. Rejoice with those who rejoice; mourn with those who mourn. Live in harmony with one another. Do not be proud, but be willing to associate with people of low position. Do not be conceited. Do not repay anyone evil for evil. Be careful to do what is right in the eyes of everyone. If it is possible, as far as it depends on you, live at peace with everyone.

Leviticus 19:18: Do not seek revenge or bear a grudge against anyone among your people, but **love your neighbor as yourself**. I am the Lord.

1 Timothy 1:5 - **The goal of this command is love**, which comes from a pure heart and a good conscience and a sincere faith.

Galatians 5:6: For in Christ Jesus neither circumcision nor uncircumcision has any value. **The only thing that counts is faith expressing itself through love.**

REVELATION CHURCHES EXHORTED TO MATURITY

Revelation 2:1-7: "To the angel of the church in Ephesus write: These are the words of him who holds the seven stars in his right hand and walks among the seven golden lampstands. I know your deeds, your hard work and your perseverance. I know that you cannot tolerate wicked people, that you have tested those who claim to be apostles but are not, and have found them false. You have persevered and have endured hardships for my name, and have not grown weary. Yet I hold this against you: You have forsaken the love you had at first. Consider how far you have fallen! Repent and do the things you did at first. If you do not repent, I will come to you and remove your lampstand from its place. But you have this in your favor: You hate the practices of the Nicolaitans, which I also hate. Whoever has ears, let them hear what the Spirit says to the churches. To the one who is victorious, I will give the right to eat from the tree of life, which is in the paradise of God.

Revelation 2:8-17: "To the angel of the church in Smyrna write: These are the words of him who is the First and the Last, who died and came to life again. I know your afflictions and your poverty – yet you are rich! I know about the slander of those who say they are Jews and are not, but are a synagogue of Satan. Do not be afraid of what you are about to suffer. I tell you, the devil will put some of you in prison to test you, and you will suffer persecution for ten days. Be faithful, even to the point of death, and I will give you life as your victor's crown. Whoever has ears, let them hear what the Spirit says to the churches. The one who is victorious will not be hurt at all by the second death. "To the angel of the church in Pergamum write: These are the words of him who has the sharp, double-edged sword. I know where you live – where Satan has his throne. Yet you remain true to my name. You did not renounce your faith in me, not even in the days of Antipas, my faithful witness, who was put to death in your city – where Satan lives. Nevertheless, I have a few things against you: There are some among you who hold to the teaching of Balaam, who taught Balak to entice the Israelites to sin so that they ate food sacrificed to idols and committed sexual immorality. Likewise, you also have those who hold to the teaching of the Nicolaitans. Repent therefore! Otherwise, I will soon come to you and will fight against them with the sword of my mouth. Whoever has ears, let them hear what the Spirit says to the churches. To the one who is victorious, I will give some of the hidden manna. I will also give that person a white stone with a new name written on it, known only to the one who receives it.

Revelation 2:18-29: "To the angel of the church in Thyatira write: These are the words of the Son of God, whose eyes are like blazing fire and whose feet are like burnished bronze. I know your deeds, your love and faith, your service and perseverance, and that you are now doing more than you did at first. Nevertheless, I have this against you: You tolerate that woman Jezebel, who calls herself a prophet. By her teaching she misleads my servants into sexual immorality and the eating of food sacrificed to idols. I have given her time to repent of her immorality, but she is unwilling. So I will cast her on a bed of suffering, and I will make those who commit adultery with her suffer intensely, unless they repent of her ways. I will strike her children dead. Then all the churches will know that I am he who searches hearts and minds, and I will repay each of you according to your deeds. Now I say to the rest of you in Thyatira, to you who do not hold to her teaching and have not learned Satan's so-called deep secrets, 'I will not impose any other burden on you, except to hold on to what you have until I come.' To the one who is victorious and does my will to the end, I will give authority over the nations – that one 'will rule them with an iron scepter and will dash them to pieces like pottery' – just as I have received authority from my Father. I will also give that one the morning star. Whoever has ears, let them hear what the Spirit says to the churches.

Revelation 3:1-6: "To the angel of the church in Sardis write: These are the words of him who holds the seven spirits of God and the seven stars. I know your deeds; you have a reputation of being alive, but you are dead. Wake up! Strengthen what remains and is about to die, for I have found your deeds unfinished in the sight of my God. Remember, therefore, what you have received and heard; hold it fast, and repent. But if you do not wake up, I will come like a thief, and you will not know at what time I will come to you. Yet you have a few people in Sardis who have not soiled their clothes. They will walk with me, dressed in white, for they are worthy. The one who is victorious will, like them, be dressed in white. I will never blot out the name of that person from the book of life, but will acknowledge that name before my Father and his angels. Whoever has ears, let them hear what the Spirit says to the churches.

Revelation 3:7-13: "To the angel of the church in Philadelphia write: These are the words of him who is holy and true, who holds the key of David. What he opens no one can shut, and what he shuts no one can open. I know your deeds. See, I have placed before you an open door that no one can shut. I know that you have little strength, yet you have kept my word and have not denied my name. I will make those who are of the synagogue of Satan, who claim to be Jews though they are not, but are liars – I will make them come and fall down at your feet and acknowledge that I have loved you. Since you have kept my command to endure patiently, I will also keep you from the hour of trial that is going to come on the whole world to test the inhabitants of the earth. I am coming soon. Hold on to what you have, so that no one will take your crown. The one who is victorious I will make a pillar in the temple of my God. Never again will they leave it. I will write on them the name of my God and the name of the city of my God, the new Jerusalem, which is coming down out of heaven from my God; and I will also write on them my new name. Whoever has ears, let them hear what the Spirit says to the churches.

Revelation 3:14-22: "To the angel of the church in Laodicea write: These are the words of the Amen, the faithful and true witness, the ruler of God's creation. I know your deeds, that you are neither cold nor hot. I wish you were either one or the other! So, because you are lukewarm – neither hot nor cold – I am about to spit you out of my mouth. You say, 'I am rich; I have acquired wealth and do not need a thing.' But you do not realize that you are wretched, pitiful, poor, blind and naked. I counsel you to buy from me gold refined in the fire, so you can become rich; and white clothes to wear, so you can cover your shameful nakedness; and salve to put on your eyes, so you can see. Those whom I love I rebuke and discipline. So be earnest and repent. Here I am! I stand at the door and knock. If anyone hears my voice and opens the door, I will come in and eat with that person, and they with me. To the one who is victorious, I will give the right to sit with me on my throne, just as I was victorious and sat down with my Father on his throne. Whoever has ears, let them hear what the Spirit says to the churches."

MATURITY FOR CHURCH LEADERSHIP

1 Timothy 3:2-12: Now **the overseer is to be above reproach**, faithful to his wife, temperate, self-controlled, respectable, hospitable, able to teach, not given to drunkenness, not violent but gentle, not quarrelsome, not a lover of money. He must manage his own family well and see that his children obey him, and he must do so in a manner worthy of full

respect. (If anyone does not know how to manage his own family, how can he take care of God's church?) He must not be a recent convert, or he may become conceited and fall under the same judgment as the devil. He must also have a good reputation with outsiders, so that he will not fall into disgrace and into the devil's trap. **In the same way, deacons are to be worthy of respect**, sincere, not indulging in much wine, and not pursuing dishonest gain. They must keep hold of the deep truths of the faith with a clear conscience. They must first be tested; and then if there is nothing against them, let them serve as deacons. In the same way, the women are to be worthy of respect, not malicious talkers but temperate and trustworthy in everything. **A deacon must be** faithful to his wife and must manage his children and his household well.

Titus 1:6-9: **An elder must be blameless**, faithful to his wife, a man whose children believe and are not open to the charge of being wild and disobedient. Since an overseer manages God's household, he must be blameless – not overbearing, not quick-tempered, not given to drunkenness, not violent, not pursuing dishonest gain. Rather, he must be hospitable, one who loves what is good, who is self-controlled, upright, holy and disciplined. He must hold firmly to the trustworthy message as it has been taught, so that he can encourage others by sound doctrine and refute those who oppose it.

Exodus 18:21: But select **capable** men from all the people – men **who fear God, trustworthy** men who hate dishonest gain – and appoint them as officials over thousands, hundreds, fifties and tens.

UNITY SCRIPTURES

Ephesians 4:1-6: Live a life worthy of the calling you have received. Be completely humble and gentle; be patient, bearing with one another in love. Make every effort to **keep the unity of the Spirit through the bond of peace**. There is **one** body and **one** Spirit, just as you were called to **one** hope when you were called; **one** Lord, **one** faith, **one** baptism; **one** God and Father of all, who is over all and through all and in all.

Philippians 2:1-2 Therefore if you have any encouragement from being united with Christ, if any comfort from his love, if any common sharing in the Spirit, if any tenderness and compassion, then make my joy complete by being **like-minded**, having the **same love**, being **one in spirit** and **of one mind**.

Psalm 133: [Living in Harmony] How good and pleasant it is when God's people live together in **unity!** It is like precious oil poured on the head, running down on the beard, running down on Aaron's beard, down on the collar of his robe. It is as if the dew of Hermon were falling on Mount Zion! For there the Lord bestows His blessing, even life forevermore.

Acts 4:32-35: [Community – One heart and mind - Sharing all possessions] All believers were **one in heart and mind**. No one claimed that any of their possessions was their own, but they shared everything they had. With great power the apostles continued to testify about the resurrection of the Lord Jesus. And God's grace was so powerfully at work in them all that there were no needy persons among them. For from time to time those who owned land or houses sold them, brought the money from the sales and put it at the apostles' feet, and it was distributed to anyone who had need.

1 Peter 3:8: All of you, be **like-minded**, be sympathetic, love one another, be compassionate and humble.

Galatians 3:26-29: So in Christ Jesus you are all children of God through faith, for all of you who were baptized into Christ have clothed yourselves with Christ. There is neither Jew nor Gentile, neither slave nor free, nor is there male and female, for **you are all one in Christ Jesus**. If you belong to Christ, then you are Abraham's seed, and heirs according to the promise.

Ephesians 2:14-22 – [One New Man: Jew and Gentile] Jesus Christ is our peace and has made the two groups one and has destroyed the barrier, the dividing wall of hostility, by setting aside in His flesh the law with its commands and regulations. **His purpose was to create in Himself one new humanity out of the two**, thus making peace, and in one Body to reconcile both of them to God through the cross, by which He **put to death their hostility**. He came and preached **peace** to you who were far away and **peace** to those who were near. For through Him we **both have access to the Father by one Spirit**. Consequently, you are no longer foreigners and strangers, but **fellow citizens with God's people and also members of His household**, built on the foundation of apostles and prophets, with Christ Jesus Himself as the chief Cornerstone. In Him the whole building is joined together and rises to become a holy temple in the Lord. And in Him you too are being built together to become a dwelling in which God lives by His Spirit.

Deuteronomy 15: [Community – fellow people of God]: If anyone is poor **among your fellow Israelites** in any of the towns of the Land the Lord your God is giving you, do not be hardhearted or tightfisted toward them. Rather, be openhanded and freely lend them whatever they need. Be careful not to harbor wicked thoughts so that you do not show ill will toward the needy among your people and give them nothing. They may then appeal to the Lord against you, and you will be found guilty of sin. Give generously to them and do so without a grudging heart; then because of this the Lord your God will bless you in all your work and in everything you set your hand to do. There will always be poor people in the land. Therefore, I command you to **be openhanded toward your fellow Israelites** who are poor and needy in the land.

Romans 12:3-8: For by the grace given me I say to every one of you: Do not think of yourself more highly than you ought, but rather think of yourself with sober judgment, in accordance with the faith God has distributed to each of you. For just as each of us has **one body with many members**, and these members do not all have the same function, so **in Christ we, though many, form one body, and each member belongs to all the others**. We have different gifts, according to the grace given to each of us. If your gift is prophesying, then prophesy in accordance with your faith; if it is serving, then serve; if it is teaching, then teach; if it is to encourage, then give encouragement; if it is giving, then give generously; if it is to lead, do it diligently; if it is to show mercy, do it cheerfully.

1 Corinthians 12:12-27: **Just as a body, though one, has many parts**, but all its many parts form one body, so it is with Christ. For we were all baptized by **one Spirit so as to form one body**—whether Jews or Gentiles, slave or free—and we were all given the one Spirit to drink. Even so the body is not made up of one part but of many. Now if the foot should say, "Because I am not a hand, I do not belong to the body," it would not for that reason stop being part of the body. And if the ear should say, "Because I am not an eye, I do not belong to the body," it would not for that reason stop being part of the body. If the whole body were an eye, where would the sense of hearing be? If the whole body were an ear, where would the sense of smell be? But in fact God has placed the parts in the body, every one of them, just as he wanted them to be. If they were all one part, where would the body be? As it is, there are many parts, but one body. The eye cannot say to the hand, "I don't need you!" And the head cannot say to the feet, "I don't need you!" On the contrary, those parts of the body that seem to be weaker are indispensable, and the parts that we think are less honorable we treat with special honor. And the parts that are unpresentable are treated with special modesty, while our presentable parts need no special treatment. But God has put the body together, giving greater honor to the parts that lacked it, so that there should be no division in the body, but that its parts should have equal concern for each other. If one part suffers, every part suffers with it; if one part is honored, every part rejoices with it. Now you are the body of Christ, and each one of you is a part of it.

JESUS PRAYER FOR DISCIPLES - THE HIGH PRIESTLY PRAYER

John 17:1-26: After Jesus said this, he looked toward heaven and prayed: "Father, the hour has come. Glorify your Son, that your Son may glorify you. For you granted him authority over all people that he might give eternal life to all those you have given him.

Now this is eternal life: **that they know you, the only true God, and Jesus Christ**, whom you have sent. I have brought you glory on earth by finishing the work you gave me to do. And now, Father, glorify me in your presence with the glory I had with you before the world began.

I have revealed you to those whom you gave me out of the world. They were yours; you gave them to me and they have obeyed your word. Now they know that everything you have given me comes from you. For I gave them the words you gave me and they accepted them. They knew with certainty that I came from you, and they believed that you sent me. I pray for them. **I am not praying for the world, but for those you have given me, for they are yours**. All I have is yours, and all you have is mine. And glory has come to me through them. I will remain in the world no longer, but they are still in the world, and I am coming to you.

Holy Father, **protect them** by the power of your name, the name you gave me, **so that they may be one as we are one**. While I was with them, I protected them and kept them safe by that name you gave me. None has been lost except the one doomed to destruction so that Scripture would be fulfilled. I am coming to you now, but I say these things while I am still in the world, so that **they may have the full measure of my joy within them**. I have given them your word and the world has hated them, for they are not of the world any more than I am of the world. **My prayer is not that you take them out of the world but that you protect them from the evil one**. They are not of the world, even as I am not of it. **Sanctify them by the truth; your word is truth**. As you sent me into the world, I have sent them into the world. For them I sanctify myself, that they too may be truly sanctified.

My prayer is not for them alone. I pray also for those who will believe in me through their message, **that all of them may be one, Father, just as you are in me and I am in you**. May they also be in us so that the world may believe that you have sent me. I have given them the glory that you gave me, **that they may be one as we are one** – I in them and you in me – **so that they may be brought to complete unity**. Then the world will know that you sent me and have loved them even as you have loved me. Father, I want those you have given me to be with me where I am, and to see my glory, the glory you have given me because you loved me before the creation of the world. Righteous Father, though the world does not know you, I know you, and they know that you have sent me. I have made you known to them, and will continue to make you known in order that the love you have for me may be in them and that I myself may be in them.

The Third Day (Tuesday)
THE NATIONS & THE DAY OF THE LORD

INDEX OF TOPICS:
- All Nations Scriptures
- Laborers in the Harvest Field
- Psalms About the Nations
- Old Testament Day of the Lord Scriptures
- New Testament Day of the Lord Scriptures
- First to the Jew, Israel & Aliyah

ALL NATIONS SCRIPTURES

Genesis 12:3: "I will bless those who bless you, and whoever curses you I will curse; and **all peoples on earth** will be blessed through you."

1 Kings 8:41-43: "As for the foreigner who does not belong to your people Israel but has come from a distant land because of your name-- for they will hear of your great name and your mighty hand and your outstretched arm--when they come and pray toward this temple, then hear from heaven, your dwelling place. Do whatever the foreigner asks of you, s**o that all the peoples of the earth may know your name and fear you**, as do your own people Israel, and may know that this house I have built bears your Name.

Psalm 22:27: "**All the ends of the earth** will remember and turn to the LORD, and all the families of the nations will bow down before him,.."

Psalm 33:8: "**Let all the earth fear the Lord**; let **all the people of the world** revere him."

Psalm 47:1: "Clap your hands, **all you nations**; shout to God with cries of joy."

Psalm 102:15: "**The nations** will fear the name of the LORD, all the kings of the earth will revere your glory."

Psalm 117:1: "Praise the LORD, **all you nations**; extol him, all you peoples."

The Third Day (Tuesday): The Nations & the Day of the Lord

Isaiah 2:2: "In the last days the mountain of the LORD's temple will be established as chief among the mountains; it will be raised above the hills, and **all nations** will stream to it."

Isaiah 45:22: "Turn to me and be saved, **all you ends of the earth**; for I am God, and there is no other."

Isaiah 45:23: "By myself I have sworn, my mouth has uttered in all integrity a word that will not be revoked: Before me **every knee will** bow; by me **every tongue will swear**."

Isaiah 49:6: "[The Lord] says: 'It is too small a thing for you to be my servant to restore the tribes of Jacob and bring back those of Israel I have kept. I will also make you a light for the Gentiles, **that you may bring my salvation to the ends of the earth**.'"

Isaiah 52:10: "The LORD will lay bare his holy arm **in the sight of all the nations**, and **all the ends of the earth** will see the salvation of our God."

Isaiah 56:7: "..these I will bring to my holy mountain and give them joy in my house of prayer. Their burnt offerings and sacrifices will be accepted on my altar; for my house will be called a **house of prayer for all nations**."

Isaiah 61:11: "For as the soil makes the sprout come up and a garden causes seeds to grow, so the Sovereign LORD will make righteousness and praise spring up before **all nations**."

Haggai 2:7: "'I will shake **all nations**, and the desired of **all nations** will come, and I will fill this house with glory,' says the LORD Almighty."

Acts 2:17a: "'In the last days,' God says, 'I will pour out my Spirit on **all people**.'"

1 John 2:2: "He is the atoning sacrifice for our sins, and not only for ours but also for the **sins of the whole world**."

Revelation 5:9: "And they sang a new song: 'You are worthy to take the scroll and to open its seals, because you were slain, and with your blood you purchased men for God from **every tribe and language and people and nation**.'"

Revelation 7:9: "After this I looked and there before me was a great multitude that no one could count, from **every nation, tribe, people and language**, standing before the throne and in front of the Lamb. They were wearing white robes and were holding palm branches in their hands."

Revelation 12:5: "She gave birth to a son, a male child, who will **rule all the nations with an iron scepter**. And her child was snatched up to God and to his throne."

Revelation 14:6-7: Then I saw another angel flying in midair, and he had the eternal gospel to proclaim to those who live on the earth--**to every nation, tribe, language and people**. He said in a loud voice, "Fear God and give him glory, because the hour of his judgment has come. Worship him who made the heavens, the earth, the sea and the springs of water."

LABORERS INTO THE HARVEST FIELD

Luke 24:46-47: He told them, "This is what is written: The Messiah will suffer and rise from the dead on the third day, and **repentance for the forgiveness of sins will be preached in his name to all nations**, beginning at Jerusalem.

Matthew 28:18-20 - Then Jesus came to them and said, "All authority in heaven and on earth has been given to me. **Therefore go and make disciples of all nations**, baptizing them in the name of the Father and of the Son and of the Holy Spirit, and teaching them to obey everything I have commanded you. And surely I am with you always, to the very end of the age."

Mark 16:15-20 - He said to them, "**Go into all the world and preach the gospel to all creation.** Whoever believes and is baptized will be saved, but whoever does not believe will be condemned. And these signs will accompany those who believe: In my name they will drive out demons; they will speak in new tongues; they will pick up snakes with their hands; and when they drink deadly poison, it will not hurt them at all; they will place their hands on sick people, and they will get well." After the Lord Jesus had spoken to them, he was taken up into heaven and he sat at the right hand of God. Then the disciples went out and preached everywhere, and the Lord worked with them and confirmed his word by the signs that accompanied it.

Matthew 9:36-38: When he saw the crowds, he had compassion on them, because they were harassed and helpless, like sheep without a shepherd. Then he said to his disciples, "The harvest is plentiful but the workers are few. **Ask the Lord of the harvest, therefore, to send out workers into his harvest field.**"

Luke 10:2-3: He told them, "The harvest is plentiful, but the workers are few. **Ask the Lord of the harvest, therefore, to send out workers into his harvest field. Go!** I am sending you out like lambs among wolves.

John 17:18: As you sent me into the world, **I have sent them into the world.**

John 20:21: Again Jesus said, "Peace be with you! **As the Father has sent me, I am sending you.**"

Acts 1:8: "'But you will receive power when the Holy Spirit comes on you; and you will be my witnesses in Jerusalem, and in all Judea and Samaria, and to the **ends of the earth.**'"

Romans 10:13-15: for, "Everyone who calls on the name of the Lord will be saved." How, then, can they call on the one they have not believed in? And how can they believe in the one of whom they have not heard? **And how can they hear without someone preaching to them? And how can anyone preach unless they are sent?** As it is written: "How beautiful are the feet of those who bring good news!"

The Third Day (Tuesday): The Nations & the Day of the Lord

1 Timothy 2:1-6: I urge, then, first of all, that petitions, prayers, intercession and thanksgiving be made for all people – for kings and all those in authority, that we may live peaceful and quiet lives in all godliness and holiness. This is good, and pleases God our Savior, **who wants all people to be saved and to come to a knowledge of the truth**. For there is one God and one mediator between God and mankind, the man Christ Jesus, who gave himself as a ransom for all people. This has now been witnessed to at the proper time.

Acts 4:24-30: When they heard this, they raised their voices together in prayer to God. "Sovereign Lord," they said, "you made the heavens and the earth and the sea, and everything in them. You spoke by the Holy Spirit through the mouth of your servant, our father David: 'Why do the nations rage and the peoples plot in vain? The kings of the earth rise up and the rulers band together against the Lord and against his anointed one.' Indeed Herod and Pontius Pilate met together with the Gentiles and the people of Israel in this city to conspire against your holy servant Jesus, whom you anointed. They did what your power and will had decided beforehand should happen. Now, Lord, consider their threats and **enable your servants to speak your word with great boldness**. Stretch out your hand to heal and perform signs and wonders through the name of your holy servant Jesus."

Mark 1:15: "The time has come," he said. "The kingdom of God has come near. **Repent and believe the good news!**"

John 3:16-18, 36: For **God so loved the world** that he gave his one and only Son, that whoever believes in him shall not perish but have eternal life. For God did not send his Son into the world to condemn the world, but to save the world through him. Whoever believes in him is not condemned, but whoever does not believe stands condemned already because they have not believed in the name of God's one and only Son. ... Whoever believes in the Son has eternal life, but whoever rejects the Son will not see life, for God's wrath remains on them.

PSALMS ABOUT THE NATIONS

Psalm 2:1-12: **Why do the nations conspire and the peoples plot in vain?** The kings of the earth rise up and the rulers band together against the LORD and against his anointed, saying, "Let us break their chains and throw off their shackles." The One enthroned in heaven laughs; the Lord scoffs at them. He rebukes them in his anger and terrifies them in his wrath, saying, "I have installed my king on Zion, my holy mountain." I will proclaim the LORD's decree: He said to me, "You are my son; today I have become your father. **Ask me, and I will make the nations your inheritance, the ends of the earth your possession**. You will break them with a rod of iron; you will dash them to pieces like pottery." Therefore, you kings, be wise; be warned, you rulers of the earth. Serve the LORD with fear and celebrate his rule with trembling. Kiss his son, or he will be angry and your way will lead to your destruction, for his wrath can flare up in a moment. Blessed are all who take refuge in him.

Psalm 9:1-20: I will give thanks to you, LORD, with all my heart; I will tell of all your wonderful deeds. I will be glad and rejoice in you; I will sing the praises of your name, O Most High.

My enemies turn back; they stumble and perish before you. For you have upheld my right and my cause, sitting enthroned as the righteous judge. **You have rebuked the nations** and destroyed the wicked; you have blotted out their name for ever and ever. Endless ruin has overtaken my enemies, you have uprooted their cities; even the memory of them has perished. The LORD reigns forever; he has established his throne for judgment. **He rules the world in righteousness and judges the peoples with equity**. The LORD is a refuge for the oppressed, a stronghold in times of trouble. Those who know your name trust in you, for you, LORD, have never forsaken those who seek you. Sing the praises of the LORD, enthroned in Zion; **proclaim among the nations what he has done**. For he who avenges blood remembers; he does not ignore the cries of the afflicted. LORD, see how my enemies persecute me! Have mercy and lift me up from the gates of death, that I may declare your praises in the gates of Daughter Zion, and there rejoice in your salvation. **The nations have fallen into the pit they have dug; their feet are caught in the net they have hidden**. The LORD is known by his acts of justice; the wicked are ensnared by the work of their hands. The wicked go down to the realm of the dead, **all the nations that forget God**. But God will never forget the needy; the hope of the afflicted will never perish. Arise, LORD, do not let mortals triumph; **let the nations be judged in your presence**. Strike them with terror, LORD; **let the nations know they are only mortal**.

Psalm 46:1-11: God is our refuge and strength, an ever-present help in trouble. Therefore we will not fear, though the earth give way and the mountains fall into the heart of the sea, though its waters roar and foam and the mountains quake with their surging. There is a river whose streams make glad the city of God, the holy place where the Most High dwells. God is within her, she will not fall; God will help her at break of day. **Nations are in uproar, kingdoms fall; he lifts his voice, the earth melts**. The LORD Almighty is with us; the God of Jacob is our fortress. Come and see what the LORD has done, the desolations he has brought on the earth. He makes wars cease to the ends of the earth. He breaks the bow and shatters the spear; he burns the shields with fire. He says, "Be still, and know that I am God; **I will be exalted among the nations, I will be exalted in the earth**." The LORD Almighty is with us; the God of Jacob is our fortress.

Psalm 67:1-7: May God be gracious to us and bless us and make his face shine on us – so that your ways may be known on earth, **your salvation among all nations**. May the peoples praise you, God; may all the peoples praise you. **May the nations be glad and sing for joy, for you rule the peoples with equity and guide the nations of the earth**. May the peoples praise you, God; may all the peoples praise you. The land yields its harvest; God, our God, blesses us. May God bless us still, **so that all the ends of the earth will fear him**.

Psalm 96:1-13: Sing to the LORD a new song; sing to the LORD, all the earth. Sing to the LORD, praise his name; proclaim his salvation day after day. **Declare his glory among the nations, his marvelous deeds among all peoples**. For great is the LORD and most worthy of praise; he is to be feared above all gods. For all the gods of the nations are idols, but the LORD made the heavens. Splendor and majesty are before him; strength and glory are in his sanctuary. Ascribe to the LORD, all you families of nations, ascribe to the LORD glory and strength. Ascribe to the LORD the glory due his name; bring an offering and come into his courts. Worship the LORD in the splendor of his holiness; tremble before him,

The Third Day (Tuesday): The Nations & the Day of the Lord

all the earth. **Say among the nations, "The LORD reigns."** The world is firmly established, it cannot be moved; he will judge the peoples with equity. Let the heavens rejoice, let the earth be glad; let the sea resound, and all that is in it. Let the fields be jubilant, and everything in them; let all the trees of the forest sing for joy. Let all creation rejoice before the LORD, for he comes, he comes to judge the earth. He will judge the world in righteousness and the peoples in his faithfulness.

Psalm 98:1-9: Sing to the LORD a new song, for he has done marvelous things; his right hand and his holy arm have worked salvation for him. **The LORD has made his salvation known and revealed his righteousness to the nations**. He has remembered his love and his faithfulness to Israel; **all the ends of the earth have seen the salvation of our God**. Shout for joy to the LORD, all the earth, burst into jubilant song with music; make music to the LORD with the harp, with the harp and the sound of singing, with trumpets and the blast of the ram's horn – shout for joy before the LORD, the King. Let the sea resound, and everything in it, the world, and all who live in it. Let the rivers clap their hands, let the mountains sing together for joy; let them sing before the LORD, for he comes to judge the earth. He will judge the world in righteousness and the peoples with equity.

Psalm 99:1-5: **The LORD reigns, let the nations tremble**; he sits enthroned between the cherubim, let the earth shake. Great is the LORD in Zion; **he is exalted over all the nations**. Let them praise your great and awesome name – he is holy. The King is mighty, he loves justice – you have established equity; in Jacob you have done what is just and right. Exalt the LORD our God and worship at his footstool; he is holy.

Psalm 115:1-18: Not to us, LORD, not to us but to your name be the glory, because of your love and faithfulness. **Why do the nations say, "Where is their God?" Our God is in heaven; he does whatever pleases him**. But their idols are silver and gold, made by human hands. They have mouths, but cannot speak, eyes, but cannot see. They have ears, but cannot hear, noses, but cannot smell. They have hands, but cannot feel, feet, but cannot walk, nor can they utter a sound with their throats. Those who make them will be like them, and so will all who trust in them. All you Israelites, trust in the LORD – he is their help and shield. House of Aaron, trust in the LORD – he is their help and shield. You who fear him, trust in the LORD – he is their help and shield. The LORD remembers us and will bless us: He will bless his people Israel, he will bless the house of Aaron, he will bless those who fear the LORD – small and great alike. May the LORD cause you to flourish, both you and your children. May you be blessed by the LORD, the Maker of heaven and earth. The highest heavens belong to the LORD, but the earth he has given to mankind. It is not the dead who praise the LORD, those who go down to the place of silence; it is we who extol the LORD, both now and forevermore. Praise the LORD.

OLD TESTAMENT DAY OF THE LORD SCRIPTURES

Amos 5:18-20: **Woe to you who long for the day of the LORD!** Why do you long for the **day of the LORD? That day** will be darkness, not light. It will be as though a man fled from a lion only to meet a bear, as though he entered his house and rested his hand on the wall only to have a snake bite him. Will not the **day of the LORD be darkness, not light – pitch-dark, without a ray of brightness?**

Joel 1:13-15: Put on sackcloth, you priests, and mourn; wail, you who minister before the altar. Come, spend the night in sackcloth, you who minister before my God; for the grain offerings and drink offerings are withheld from the house of your God. Declare a holy fast; call a sacred assembly. Summon the elders and all who live in the land to the house of the LORD your God, and cry out to the LORD. **Alas for that day!** For the **day of the LORD** is near; it will come like destruction from the Almighty.

Joel 2:1-17, 30-32: Blow the trumpet in Zion; sound the alarm on my holy hill. Let all who live in the land tremble, for the **day of the LORD** is coming. It is close at hand – **a day of darkness and gloom, a day of clouds and blackness.** Like dawn spreading across the mountains a large and mighty army comes, such as never was in ancient times nor ever will be in ages to come. Before them fire devours, behind them a flame blazes. Before them the land is like the garden of Eden, behind them, a desert waste – nothing escapes them. They have the appearance of horses; they gallop along like cavalry. With a noise like that of chariots they leap over the mountaintops, like a crackling fire consuming stubble, like a mighty army drawn up for battle. At the sight of them, nations are in anguish; every face turns pale. They charge like warriors; they scale walls like soldiers. They all march in line, not swerving from their course. They do not jostle each other; each marches straight ahead. They plunge through defenses without breaking ranks. They rush upon the city; they run along the wall. They climb into the houses; like thieves they enter through the windows. Before them the earth shakes, the heavens tremble, the sun and moon are darkened, and the stars no longer shine. The LORD thunders at the head of his army; his forces are beyond number, and mighty is the army that obeys his command. **The day of the LORD is great; it is dreadful. Who can endure it?** "Even now," declares the LORD, "return to me with all your heart, with fasting and weeping and mourning." Rend your heart and not your garments. Return to the LORD your God, for he is gracious and compassionate, slow to anger and abounding in love, and he relents from sending calamity. Who knows? He may turn and relent and leave behind a blessing – grain offerings and drink offerings for the LORD your God. Blow the trumpet in Zion, declare a holy fast, call a sacred assembly. Gather the people, consecrate the assembly; bring together the elders, gather the children, those nursing at the breast. Let the bridegroom leave his room and the bride her chamber. Let the priests, who minister before the LORD, weep between the portico and the altar. Let them say, "Spare your people, LORD. Do not make your inheritance an object of scorn, a byword among the nations. Why should they say among the peoples, 'Where is their God?' " ... I will show wonders in the heavens and on the earth, blood and fire and billows of smoke. The sun will be turned to darkness and the moon to blood before the coming of the **great and dreadful day of the LORD**. And everyone who calls on the name of the LORD will be saved; for on Mount Zion and in Jerusalem there will be deliverance, as the LORD has said, even among the survivors whom the LORD calls.

Joel 3:12-21: "Let the nations be roused; let them advance into the Valley of Jehoshaphat, for there I will sit to judge all the nations on every side. Swing the sickle, for the harvest is ripe. Come, trample the grapes, for the winepress is full and the vats overflow – so great is

The Third Day (Tuesday): The Nations & the Day of the Lord

their wickedness!" Multitudes, multitudes in the valley of decision! For the **day of the LORD** is near in the valley of decision. The sun and moon will be darkened, and the stars no longer shine. The LORD will roar from Zion and thunder from Jerusalem; the earth and the heavens will tremble. But the LORD will be a refuge for his people, a stronghold for the people of Israel. "Then you will know that I, the LORD your God, dwell in Zion, my holy hill. Jerusalem will be holy; never again will foreigners invade her. "**In that day** the mountains will drip new wine, and the hills will flow with milk; all the ravines of Judah will run with water. A fountain will flow out of the LORD's house and will water the valley of acacias. But Egypt will be desolate, Edom a desert waste, because of violence done to the people of Judah, in whose land they shed innocent blood. Judah will be inhabited forever and Jerusalem through all generations. Shall I leave their innocent blood unavenged? No, I will not." The LORD dwells in Zion!

Zephaniah 1:7-18: **Be silent before the Sovereign LORD, for the day of the LORD is near**. The LORD has prepared a sacrifice; he has consecrated those he has invited. "On the **day of the LORD's sacrifice** I will punish the officials and the king's sons and all those clad in foreign clothes. **On that day** I will punish all who avoid stepping on the threshold, who fill the temple of their gods with violence and deceit. "**On that day**," declares the LORD, "a cry will go up from the Fish Gate, wailing from the New Quarter, and a loud crash from the hills. Wail, you who live in the market district; all your merchants will be wiped out, all who trade with silver will be destroyed. **At that time** I will search Jerusalem with lamps and punish those who are complacent, who are like wine left on its dregs, who think, 'The LORD will do nothing, either good or bad.' Their wealth will be plundered, their houses demolished. Though they build houses, they will not live in them; though they plant vineyards, they will not drink the wine." **The great day of the LORD** is near – near and coming quickly. **The cry on the day of the LORD is bitter**; the Mighty Warrior shouts his battle cry. **That day will be a day of wrath – a day of distress and anguish, a day of trouble and ruin, a day of darkness and gloom, a day of clouds and blackness** – a day of trumpet and battle cry against the fortified cities and against the corner towers. "I will bring such distress on all people that they will grope about like those who are blind, because they have sinned against the LORD. Their blood will be poured out like dust and their entrails like dung. Neither their silver nor their gold will be able to save them on the **day of the LORD's wrath**." In the fire of his jealousy the whole earth will be consumed, for he will make a sudden end of all who live on the earth.

Zephaniah 2:1-3: Gather together, gather yourselves together, you shameful nation, before the decree takes effect and that day passes like windblown chaff, before the LORD's fierce anger comes upon you, before the **day of the LORD's wrath** comes upon you. Seek the LORD, all you humble of the land, you who do what he commands. Seek righteousness, seek humility; perhaps you will be sheltered on the **day of the LORD's anger**.

Isaiah 13:6-13: **Wail, for the day of the LORD is near**; it will come like destruction from the Almighty. Because of this, all hands will go limp, every heart will melt with fear. Terror will seize them, pain and anguish will grip them; they will writhe like a woman in labor. They will look aghast at each other, their faces aflame. See, the **day of the LORD** is coming – a cruel day, with wrath and fierce anger – to make the land desolate and destroy the sinners within it. The stars of heaven and their constellations will not show their light. The rising sun will be darkened and the moon will not give its light. I will punish the world for its evil, the wicked for their sins. I will put an end to the arrogance of the haughty and will humble the pride of the ruthless. I will make people scarcer than pure gold, more rare than the gold of Ophir. Therefore I will make the heavens tremble; and the earth will shake from its place at the wrath of the LORD Almighty, **in the day of his burning anger**.

Jeremiah 46:10-12: But **that day belongs to the Lord, the LORD Almighty – a day of vengeance, for vengeance on his foes**. The sword will devour till it is satisfied, till it has quenched its thirst with blood. For the Lord, the LORD Almighty, will offer sacrifice in the land of the north by the River Euphrates. "Go up to Gilead and get balm, Virgin Daughter Egypt. But you try many medicines in vain; there is no healing for you. The nations will hear of your shame; your cries will fill the earth. One warrior will stumble over another; both will fall down together."

Ezekiel 30:2-3: "Son of man, prophesy and say: 'This is what the Sovereign LORD says: 'Wail and say, **"Alas for that day!"** For the day is near, the **day of the LORD** is near – a day of clouds, a time of doom for the nations.

Ezekiel 13:2-5: Son of man, prophesy against the prophets of Israel who are now prophesying. Say to those who prophesy out of their own imagination: 'Hear the word of the LORD! This is what the Sovereign LORD says: Woe to the foolish prophets who follow their own spirit and have seen nothing! Your prophets, Israel, are like jackals among ruins. You have not gone up to the breaches in the wall to repair it for the people of Israel **so that it will stand firm in the battle on the day of the LORD**.

Obadiah 1:15-17: 'The **day of the LORD is near for all nations**. As you have done, it will be done to you; your deeds will return upon your own head. Just as you drank on my holy hill, so all the nations will drink continually; they will drink and drink and be as if they had never been. But on Mount Zion will be deliverance; it will be holy, and Jacob will possess his inheritance.

Malachi 4:1-6: "**Surely the day is coming; it will burn like a furnace. All the arrogant and every evildoer will be stubble, and the day that is coming will set them on fire**," says the LORD Almighty. "Not a root or a branch will be left to them. But for you who revere my name, the sun of righteousness will rise with healing in its rays. And you will go out and frolic like well-fed calves. Then you will trample on the wicked; they will be ashes under the soles of your feet on the day when I act," says the LORD Almighty. "Remember the law of my servant Moses, the decrees and laws I gave him at Horeb for all Israel. "See, I will send the prophet Elijah to you before that **great and dreadful day of the LORD** comes. He will turn the hearts of the parents to their children, and the hearts of the children to their parents; or else I will come and strike the land with total destruction."

Isaiah 2:11-22: The eyes of the arrogant will be humbled and human pride brought low; the LORD alone will be exalted **in that day. The LORD Almighty has a day in store for all the proud and lofty**, for all that is exalted (and they will be humbled), for all the cedars of Lebanon, tall and lofty, and all the oaks of Bashan, for all the towering mountains and all the high hills, for every lofty tower and every fortified wall, for every trading ship and every stately vessel. The arrogance of man will be brought low and human pride humbled; **the LORD alone will be exalted in that day**, and the idols will totally disappear. People will flee to caves in the rocks and to holes in the ground from the fearful presence of the LORD and the splendor of his majesty, when he rises to shake the earth. **In that day** people will throw away to the moles and bats their idols of silver and idols of gold, which they made to worship. They will flee to caverns in the rocks and to the overhanging crags from the fearful presence of the LORD and the splendor of his majesty, when he rises to shake the earth. Stop trusting in mere humans, who have but a breath in their nostrils. Why hold them in esteem?

Isaiah 11:10-12: **In that day** the Root of Jesse will stand as a banner for the peoples; the nations will rally to him, and his resting place will be glorious. **In that day** the Lord will reach out his hand a second time to reclaim the surviving remnant of his people from Assyria, from Lower Egypt, from Upper Egypt, from Cush, from Elam, from Babylonia, from Hamath and from the islands of the Mediterranean. He will raise a banner for the nations and gather the exiles of Israel; he will assemble the scattered people of Judah from the four quarters of the earth.

Isaiah 24:17-23: Terror and pit and snare await you, people of the earth. Whoever flees at the sound of terror will fall into a pit; whoever climbs out of the pit will be caught in a snare. The floodgates of the heavens are opened, the foundations of the earth shake. The earth is broken up, the earth is split asunder, the earth is violently shaken. The earth reels like a drunkard, it sways like a hut in the wind; so heavy upon it is the guilt of its rebellion that it falls – never to rise again. **In that day the LORD will punish the powers in the heavens above and the kings on the earth below**. They will be herded together like prisoners bound in a dungeon; they will be shut up in prison and be punished after many days. The moon will be dismayed, the sun ashamed; for the LORD Almighty will reign on Mount Zion and in Jerusalem, and before its elders – with great glory.

Isaiah 25:6-9: On this mountain the LORD Almighty will prepare a feast of rich food for all peoples, a banquet of aged wine – the best of meats and the finest of wines. On this mountain he will destroy the shroud that enfolds all peoples, the sheet that covers all nations; he will swallow up death forever. The Sovereign LORD will wipe away the tears from all faces; he will remove his people's disgrace from all the earth. The LORD has spoken. **In that day they will say, "Surely this is our God; we trusted in him, and he saved us. This is the LORD, we trusted in him; let us rejoice and be glad in his salvation."**

Isaiah 27:1-5, 12-13: **In that day**, the LORD will punish with his sword – his fierce, great and powerful sword – Leviathan the gliding serpent, Leviathan the coiling serpent; he will slay the monster of the sea. **In that day** – "Sing about a fruitful vineyard: I, the LORD, watch over it; I water it continually. I guard it day and night so that no one may harm it. I am not angry. If only there were briers and thorns confronting me! I would march against them in battle; I would set them all on fire. Or else let them come to me for refuge; let them make peace with me, yes, let them make peace with me." ...**In that day** the LORD will thresh from the flowing Euphrates to the Wadi of Egypt, and you, Israel, will be gathered up one by one. And **in that day** a great trumpet will sound. Those who were perishing in Assyria and those who were exiled in Egypt will come and worship the LORD on the holy mountain in Jerusalem.

Zechariah 12:1-14: A prophecy: The word of the LORD concerning Israel. The LORD, who stretches out the heavens, who lays the foundation of the earth, and who forms the human spirit within a person, declares: "I am going to make Jerusalem a cup that sends all the surrounding peoples reeling. Judah will be besieged as well as Jerusalem. **On that day**, when all the nations of the earth are gathered against her, I will make Jerusalem an immovable rock for all the nations. All who try to move it will injure themselves. **On that day** I will strike every horse with panic and its rider with madness," declares the LORD. "I will keep a watchful eye over Judah, but I will blind all the horses of the nations. Then the clans of Judah will say in their hearts, 'The people of Jerusalem are strong, because the LORD Almighty is their God.' "**On that day** I will make the clans of Judah like a firepot in a woodpile, like a flaming torch among sheaves. They will consume all the surrounding peoples right and left, but Jerusalem will remain intact in her place. "The LORD will save the dwellings of Judah first, so that the honor of the house of David and of Jerusalem's inhabitants may not be greater than that of Judah. **On that day** the LORD will shield those who live in Jerusalem, so that the feeblest among them will be like David, and the house of David will be like God, like the angel of the LORD going before them. **On that day** I will set out to destroy all the nations that attack Jerusalem. "And I will pour out on the house of David and the inhabitants of Jerusalem a spirit of grace and supplication. They will look on me, the one they have pierced, and they will mourn for him as one mourns for an only child, and grieve bitterly for him as one grieves for a firstborn son. **On that day** the weeping in Jerusalem will be as great as the weeping of Hadad Rimmon in the plain of Megiddo. The land will mourn, each clan by itself, with their wives by themselves: the clan of the house of David and their wives, the clan of the house of Nathan and their wives, the clan of the house of Levi and their wives, the clan of Shimei and their wives, and all the rest of the clans and their wives.

Zechariah 13:1-9: "**On that day** a fountain will be opened to the house of David and the inhabitants of Jerusalem, to cleanse them from sin and impurity. "**On that day**, I will banish the names of the idols from the land, and they will be remembered no more," declares the LORD Almighty. "I will remove both the prophets and the spirit of impurity from the land. And if anyone still prophesies, their father and mother, to whom they were born, will say to them, 'You must die, because you have told lies in the LORD's name.' Then their own parents will stab the one who prophesies. "**On that day** every prophet will be ashamed of their prophetic vision. They will not put on a prophet's garment of hair in order to deceive. Each will say, 'I am not a prophet. I am a farmer; the land has been my livelihood since my youth.' If someone asks, 'What are these wounds on your body?' they will answer, 'The wounds I was given at the house of my friends.' "Awake, sword, against my shepherd, against the man who is close to me!" declares the LORD Almighty. "Strike the shepherd, and the sheep will be scattered, and I will turn my hand against the little ones. In the whole land," declares the LORD, "two-thirds will be struck down and perish; yet one-third will be left in it. This third I will put into the fire; I will refine them like silver and test them like gold. They will call on my name and I will answer them; I will say, 'They are my people,' and they will say, 'The LORD is our God.'"

The Third Day (Tuesday): The Nations & the Day of the Lord

Zechariah 14:1-16: **A day of the LORD is coming**, Jerusalem, when your possessions will be plundered and divided up within your very walls. I will gather all the nations to Jerusalem to fight against it; the city will be captured, the houses ransacked, and the women raped. Half of the city will go into exile, but the rest of the people will not be taken from the city. Then the LORD will go out and fight against those nations, as he fights on a day of battle. **On that day** his feet will stand on the Mount of Olives, east of Jerusalem, and the Mount of Olives will be split in two from east to west, forming a great valley, with half of the mountain moving north and half moving south. You will flee by my mountain valley, for it will extend to Azel. You will flee as you fled from the earthquake in the days of Uzziah king of Judah. Then the LORD my God will come, and all the holy ones with him. **On that day** there will be neither sunlight nor cold, frosty darkness. **It will be a unique day – a day known only to the LORD – with no distinction between day and night.** When evening comes, there will be light. **On that day** living water will flow out from Jerusalem, half of it east to the Dead Sea and half of it west to the Mediterranean Sea, in summer and in winter. The LORD will be king over the whole earth. **On that day** there will be one LORD, and his name the only name. The whole land, from Geba to Rimmon, south of Jerusalem, will become like the Arabah. But Jerusalem will be raised up high from the Benjamin Gate to the site of the First Gate, to the Corner Gate, and from the Tower of Hananel to the royal winepresses, and will remain in its place. It will be inhabited; never again will it be destroyed. Jerusalem will be secure. **This is the plague with which the LORD will strike all the nations that fought against Jerusalem: Their flesh will rot while they are still standing on their feet, their eyes will rot in their sockets, and their tongues will rot in their mouths. On that day people will be stricken by the LORD with great panic.** They will seize each other by the hand and attack one another. Judah too will fight at Jerusalem. The wealth of all the surrounding nations will be collected – great quantities of gold and silver and clothing. A similar plague will strike the horses and mules, the camels and donkeys, and all the animals in those camps. Then the survivors from all the nations that have attacked Jerusalem will go up year after year to worship the King, the LORD Almighty, and to celebrate the Festival of Tabernacles.

Ezekiel 18:23, 29-32: **Do I take any pleasure in the death of the wicked?** declares the Sovereign LORD. Rather, am I not pleased when they turn from their ways and live? ... Yet the Israelites say, 'The way of the Lord is not just.' Are my ways unjust, people of Israel? Is it not your ways that are unjust? "Therefore, you Israelites, I will judge each of you according to your own ways, declares the Sovereign LORD. **Repent! Turn away from all your offenses; then sin will not be your downfall.** Rid yourselves of all the offenses you have committed, and get a new heart and a new spirit. Why will you die, people of Israel? For I take no pleasure in the death of anyone, declares the Sovereign LORD. **Repent and live!**

NEW TESTAMENT DAY OF THE LORD SCRIPTURES

Matthew 24:3-42: As Jesus was sitting on the Mount of Olives, the disciples came to him privately. "Tell us," they said, "when will this happen, and **what will be the sign of your coming and of the end of the age?**"

Jesus answered: "Watch out that no one deceives you. For many will come in my name, claiming, 'I am the Messiah,' and will deceive many. You will hear of wars and rumors of wars, but see to it that you are not alarmed. Such things must happen, but the end is still to come. **Nation will rise against nation, and kingdom against kingdom**. There will be famines and earthquakes in various places. All these are the beginning of birth pains.

"Then you will be handed over to be persecuted and put to death, and **you will be hated by all nations because of me**. At that time many will turn away from the faith and will betray and hate each other, and many false prophets will appear and deceive many people. Because of the increase of wickedness, the love of most will grow cold, but the one who stands firm to the end will be saved. **And this gospel of the kingdom will be preached in the whole world as a testimony to all nations, and then the end will come**. "So when you see standing in the holy place 'the abomination that causes desolation,' spoken of through the prophet Daniel – let the reader understand – then let those who are in Judea flee to the mountains. Let no one on the housetop go down to take anything out of the house. Let no one in the field go back to get their cloak. How dreadful it will be in those days for pregnant women and nursing mothers! Pray that your flight will not take place in winter or on the Sabbath. For then there will be great distress, unequaled from the beginning of the world until now – and never to be equaled again. "If those days had not been cut short, no one would survive, but for the sake of the elect those days will be shortened. At that time if anyone says to you, 'Look, here is the Messiah!' or, 'There he is!' do not believe it. For false messiahs and false prophets will appear and perform great signs and wonders to deceive, if possible, even the elect. See, I have told you ahead of time. "So if anyone tells you, 'There he is, out in the wilderness,' do not go out; or, 'Here he is, in the inner rooms,' do not believe it. For as lightning that comes from the east is visible even in the west, so will be the coming of the Son of Man. Wherever there is a carcass, there the vultures will gather.

"Immediately after the distress of those days 'the sun will be darkened, and the moon will not give its light; the stars will fall from the sky, and the heavenly bodies will be shaken.' **"Then will appear the sign of the Son of Man in heaven**. And then all the peoples of the earth will mourn when they see the Son of Man coming on the clouds of heaven, with power and great glory. And he will send his angels with a loud trumpet call, and they will gather his elect from the four winds, from one end of the heavens to the other. "Now learn this lesson from the fig tree: As soon as its twigs get tender and its leaves come out, you know that summer is near. **Even so, when you see all these things, you know that it is near, right at the door**. Truly I tell you, this generation will certainly not pass away until all these things have happened. Heaven and earth will pass away, but my words will never pass away. "**But about that day or hour no one knows, not even the angels in heaven, nor the Son, but only the Father**. As it was in the days of Noah, so it will be at the coming of the Son of Man. For in the days before the flood, people were eating and drinking, marrying and giving in marriage, up to the day Noah entered the ark; and they knew nothing about what would happen until the flood came and took them all away. **That is how it will be at the coming of the Son of Man**. Two men will be in the field; one will be taken and the other left. Two women will be grinding with a hand mill; one will be taken and the other left. "Therefore keep watch, because you do not know on what day your Lord will come.
See also Mark 13; Luke 12, 21.

The Third Day (Tuesday): The Nations & the Day of the Lord

2 Thessalonians 2:1-12: **Concerning the coming of our Lord Jesus Christ** and our being gathered to him, we ask you, brothers and sisters, not to become easily unsettled or alarmed by the teaching allegedly from us – whether by a prophecy or by word of mouth or by letter – asserting that the **day of the Lord** has already come. Don't let anyone deceive you in any way, for **that day** will not come until the rebellion occurs and the man of lawlessness is revealed, the man doomed to destruction. He will oppose and will exalt himself over everything that is called God or is worshiped, so that he sets himself up in God's temple, proclaiming himself to be God. Don't you remember that when I was with you I used to tell you these things? And now you know what is holding him back, so that he may be revealed at the proper time. For the secret power of lawlessness is already at work; but the one who now holds it back will continue to do so till he is taken out of the way. And then the lawless one will be revealed, whom the Lord Jesus will overthrow with the breath of his mouth and destroy by the splendor of his coming. The coming of the lawless one will be in accordance with how Satan works. He will use all sorts of displays of power through signs and wonders that serve the lie, and all the ways that wickedness deceives those who are perishing. They perish because they refused to love the truth and so be saved. For this reason God sends them a powerful delusion so that they will believe the lie and so that all will be condemned who have not believed the truth but have delighted in wickedness.

2 Thessalonians 1:6-10: God is just: He will pay back trouble to those who trouble you and give relief to you who are troubled, and to us as well. This will happen **when the Lord Jesus is revealed from heaven in blazing fire with his powerful angels**. He will punish those who do not know God and do not obey the gospel of our Lord Jesus. They will be punished with everlasting destruction and shut out from the presence of the Lord and from the glory of his might on the day he comes to be glorified in his holy people and to be marveled at among all those who have believed. This includes you, because you believed our testimony to you.

1 Thessalonians 4:15-5:4:- According to the Lord's word, we tell you that we who are still alive, who are left **until the coming of the Lord**, will certainly not precede those who have fallen asleep. For **the Lord himself will come down from heaven, with a loud command, with the voice of the archangel and with the trumpet call of God**, and the dead in Christ will rise first. After that, we who are still alive and are left will be caught up together with them in the clouds to meet the Lord in the air. And so we will be with the Lord forever. Therefore encourage one another with these words. Now, brothers and sisters, **about times and dates we do not need to write to you, for you know very well that the day of the Lord will come like a thief in the night**. While people are saying, "Peace and safety," destruction will come on them suddenly, as labor pains on a pregnant woman, and they will not escape. But you, brothers and sisters, are not in darkness so that this day should surprise you like a thief.

2 Peter 3:3-12: Above all, you must understand that **in the last days** scoffers will come, scoffing and following their own evil desires. They will say, "Where is this 'coming' he promised? Ever since our ancestors died, everything goes on as it has since the beginning of creation." But they deliberately forget that long ago by God's word the heavens came

into being and the earth was formed out of water and by water. By these waters also the world of that time was deluged and destroyed. By the same word the present heavens and earth are reserved for fire, being kept for the day of judgment and destruction of the ungodly. But do not forget this one thing, dear friends: With the Lord a day is like a thousand years, and a thousand years are like a day. The Lord is not slow in keeping his promise, as some understand slowness. Instead he is patient with you, not wanting anyone to perish, but everyone to come to repentance. **But the day of the Lord will come like a thief**. The heavens will disappear with a roar; the elements will be destroyed by fire, and the earth and everything done in it will be laid bare. Since everything will be destroyed in this way, what kind of people ought you to be? You ought to live holy and godly lives as you look forward to the day of God and speed its coming. **That day** will bring about the destruction of the heavens by fire, and the elements will melt in the heat.

2 Timothy 4:1-5: In the presence of God and of Christ Jesus, who will judge the living and the dead, and **in view of his appearing and his kingdom**, I give you this charge: Preach the word; be prepared in season and out of season; correct, rebuke and encourage – with great patience and careful instruction. For the time will come when people will not put up with sound doctrine. Instead, to suit their own desires, they will gather around them a great number of teachers to say what their itching ears want to hear. They will turn their ears away from the truth and turn aside to myths. But you, keep your head in all situations, endure hardship, do the work of an evangelist, discharge all the duties of your ministry.

1 John 2:18-22: Dear children, **this is the last hour**; and as you have heard that the antichrist is coming, even now many antichrists have come. This is how we know it is the last hour. They went out from us, but they did not really belong to us. For if they had belonged to us, they would have remained with us; but their going showed that none of them belonged to us. But you have an anointing from the Holy One, and all of you know the truth. I do not write to you because you do not know the truth, but because you do know it and because no lie comes from the truth. Who is the liar? It is whoever denies that Jesus is the Christ. Such a person is the antichrist – denying the Father and the Son.

Matthew 7:21-23: "Not everyone who says to me, 'Lord, Lord,' will enter the kingdom of heaven, but only the one who does the will of my Father who is in heaven. Many will say to me **on that day**, 'Lord, Lord, did we not prophesy in your name and in your name drive out demons and in your name perform many miracles?' Then I will tell them plainly, 'I never knew you. Away from me, you evildoers!'

Philippians 1:6: being confident of this, that he who began a good work in you will carry it on to completion **until the day of Christ Jesus**.

Revelation 13:1-10: The dragon stood on the shore of the sea. And I saw a beast coming out of the sea. It had ten horns and seven heads, with ten crowns on its horns, and on each head a blasphemous name. The beast I saw resembled a leopard, but had feet like those of a bear and a mouth like that of a lion. The dragon gave the beast his power and his throne and great authority. One of the heads of the beast seemed to have had a fatal wound, but the fatal wound had been healed. The whole world was filled with wonder

The Third Day (Tuesday): The Nations & the Day of the Lord

and followed the beast. People worshiped the dragon because he had given authority to the beast, and they also worshiped the beast and asked, "Who is like the beast? Who can wage war against it?" The beast was given a mouth to utter proud words and blasphemies and to exercise its authority for forty-two months. It opened its mouth to blaspheme God, and to slander his name and his dwelling place and those who live in heaven. It was given power to wage war against God's holy people and to conquer them. And it was given authority over every tribe, people, language and nation. All inhabitants of the earth will worship the beast – all whose names have not been written in the Lamb's book of life, the Lamb who was slain from the creation of the world. Whoever has ears, let them hear. "If anyone is to go into captivity, into captivity they will go. If anyone is to be killed with the sword, with the sword they will be killed." This calls for patient endurance and faithfulness on the part of God's people.

Revelation 18:2-24: With a mighty voice he shouted: "**Fallen! Fallen is Babylon the Great**! She has become a dwelling for demons and a haunt for every impure spirit, a haunt for every unclean bird, a haunt for every unclean and detestable animal. For all the nations have drunk the maddening wine of her adulteries. The kings of the earth committed adultery with her, and the merchants of the earth grew rich from her excessive luxuries." Then I heard another voice from heaven say: "'**Come out of her, my people**, so that you will not share in her sins, so that you will not receive any of her plagues; for her sins are piled up to heaven, and God has remembered her crimes. Give back to her as she has given; pay her back double for what she has done. Pour her a double portion from her own cup. Give her as much torment and grief as the glory and luxury she gave herself. In her heart she boasts, 'I sit enthroned as queen. I am not a widow; I will never mourn.' Therefore in one day her plagues will overtake her: death, mourning and famine. She will be consumed by fire, for mighty is the Lord God who judges her. "When the kings of the earth who committed adultery with her and shared her luxury see the smoke of her burning, they will weep and mourn over her. Terrified at her torment, they will stand far off and cry: '**Woe! Woe to you, great city, you mighty city of Babylon! In one hour your doom has come!**' "The merchants of the earth will weep and mourn over her because no one buys their cargoes anymore – cargoes of gold, silver, precious stones and pearls; fine linen, purple, silk and scarlet cloth; every sort of citron wood, and articles of every kind made of ivory, costly wood, bronze, iron and marble; cargoes of cinnamon and spice, of incense, myrrh and frankincense, of wine and olive oil, of fine flour and wheat; cattle and sheep; horses and carriages; and human beings sold as slaves. "They will say, 'The fruit you longed for is gone from you. All your luxury and splendor have vanished, never to be recovered.' The merchants who sold these things and gained their wealth from her will stand far off, terrified at her torment. They will weep and mourn and cry out: '**Woe! Woe to you, great city**, dressed in fine linen, purple and scarlet, and glittering with gold, precious stones and pearls! In one hour such great wealth has been brought to ruin!' "Every sea captain, and all who travel by ship, the sailors, and all who earn their living from the sea, will stand far off. When they see the smoke of her burning, they will exclaim, 'Was there ever a city like this great city?' They will throw dust on their heads, and with weeping and mourning cry out: '**Woe! Woe to you, great city**, where all who had ships on the sea became rich through her wealth! In one hour she has been brought to ruin!' "**Rejoice over her, you heavens! Rejoice, you people of God! Rejoice, apostles and prophets! For God has judged her with**

the judgment she imposed on you." Then a mighty angel picked up a boulder the size of a large millstone and threw it into the sea, and said: "With such violence the great city of Babylon will be thrown down, never to be found again. The music of harpists and musicians, pipers and trumpeters, will never be heard in you again. No worker of any trade will ever be found in you again. The sound of a millstone will never be heard in you again. The light of a lamp will never shine in you again. The voice of bridegroom and bride will never be heard in you again. Your merchants were the world's important people. By your magic spell [pharmakeia] all the nations were led astray. In her was found the blood of prophets and of God's holy people, of all who have been slaughtered on the earth."

Revelation 19:1-9: After this I heard what sounded like the roar of a great multitude in heaven shouting: "**Hallelujah! Salvation and glory and power belong to our God, for true and just are his judgments**. He has condemned the great prostitute who corrupted the earth by her adulteries. He has avenged on her the blood of his servants." And again they shouted: "**Hallelujah! The smoke from her goes up for ever and ever.**" The twenty-four elders and the four living creatures fell down and worshiped God, who was seated on the throne. And they cried: "**Amen, Hallelujah!**" Then a voice came from the throne, saying: "Praise our God, all you his servants, you who fear him, both great and small!" Then I heard what sounded like a great multitude, like the roar of rushing waters and like loud peals of thunder, shouting: "**Hallelujah! For our Lord God Almighty reigns. Let us rejoice and be glad and give him glory! For the wedding of the Lamb has come, and his bride has made herself ready**. Fine linen, bright and clean, was given her to wear." (Fine linen stands for the righteous acts of God's holy people.) Then the angel said to me, "Write this: Blessed are those who are invited to the wedding supper of the Lamb!" And he added, "These are the true words of God."

Revelation 19:11-16: I saw heaven standing open and there before me was a white horse, whose rider is called Faithful and True. With justice he judges and wages war. His eyes are like blazing fire, and on his head are many crowns. He has a name written on him that no one knows but he himself. He is dressed in a robe dipped in blood, and his name is the Word of God. The armies of heaven were following him, riding on white horses and dressed in fine linen, white and clean. **Coming out of his mouth is a sharp sword with which to strike down the nations. "He will rule them with an iron scepter**." He treads the winepress of the fury of the wrath of God Almighty. On his robe and on his thigh he has this name written: king of kings and lord of lords.

FIRST TO THE JEW, ISRAEL, AND ALIYAH

Romans 1:16-17: For I am not ashamed of the gospel, because it is the power of God that brings salvation to everyone who believes: **first to the Jew**, then to the Gentile. For in the gospel the righteousness of God is revealed – a righteousness that is by faith from first to last, just as it is written: "The righteous will live by faith."

Romans 2:6-11: God "will repay each person according to what they have done." To those who by persistence in doing good seek glory, honor and immortality, he will give eternal

The Third Day (Tuesday): The Nations & the Day of the Lord

life. But for those who are self-seeking and who reject the truth and follow evil, there will be wrath and anger. There will be trouble and distress for every human being who does evil: **first for the Jew**, then for the Gentile; but glory, honor and peace for everyone who does good: **first for the Jew**, then for the Gentile. For God does not show favoritism.

Romans 11:1-12: I ask then: **Did God reject his people? By no means!** I am an Israelite myself, a descendant of Abraham, from the tribe of Benjamin. **God did not reject his people, whom he foreknew.** Don't you know what Scripture says in the passage about Elijah – how he appealed to God against Israel: "Lord, they have killed your prophets and torn down your altars; I am the only one left, and they are trying to kill me"? And what was God's answer to him? "I have reserved for myself seven thousand who have not bowed the knee to Baal." **So too, at the present time there is a remnant chosen by grace.** And if by grace, then it cannot be based on works; if it were, grace would no longer be grace. What then? What the people of Israel sought so earnestly they did not obtain. The elect among them did, but the others were hardened, as it is written: "God gave them a spirit of stupor, eyes that could not see and ears that could not hear, to this very day." And David says: "May their table become a snare and a trap, a stumbling block and a retribution for them. May their eyes be darkened so they cannot see, and their backs be bent forever." Again I ask: **Did they stumble so as to fall beyond recovery? Not at all!** Rather, because of their transgression, salvation has come to the Gentiles to **make Israel envious**. But if their transgression means riches for the world, and their loss means riches for the Gentiles, how much greater riches will **their full inclusion** bring!

Romans 11:25-36: I do not want you to be ignorant of this mystery, brothers and sisters, so that you may not be conceited: **Israel has experienced a hardening in part until the full number of the Gentiles has come in, and in this way all Israel will be saved**. As it is written: "The deliverer will come from Zion; he will turn godlessness away from Jacob. And this is my covenant with them when I take away their sins." As far as the gospel is concerned, they are enemies for your sake; but **as far as election is concerned, they are loved on account of the patriarchs, for God's gifts and his call are irrevocable**. Just as you who were at one time disobedient to God have now received mercy as a result of their disobedience, so they too have now become disobedient in order that they too may now receive mercy as a result of God's mercy to you. For God has bound everyone over to disobedience so that he may have mercy on them all. Oh, the depth of the riches of the wisdom and knowledge of God! How unsearchable his judgments, and his paths beyond tracing out! "Who has known the mind of the Lord? Or who has been his counselor?" "Who has ever given to God, that God should repay them?" For from him and through him and for him are all things. To him be the glory forever! Amen.

The Song of Moses (excerpt):
Deuteronomy 32:18-43: You deserted the Rock, who fathered you; you forgot the God who gave you birth. The LORD saw this and rejected them because he was angered by his sons and daughters. "I will hide my face from them," he said, "and see what their end will be; for they are a perverse generation, children who are unfaithful. They made me jealous by what is no god and angered me with their worthless idols. **I will make them envious by those who are not a people**; I will make them angry by a nation that has no

understanding. For a fire will be kindled by my wrath, one that burns down to the realm of the dead below. It will devour the earth and its harvests and set afire the foundations of the mountains. "I will heap calamities on them and spend my arrows against them. I will send wasting famine against them, consuming pestilence and deadly plague; I will send against them the fangs of wild beasts, the venom of vipers that glide in the dust. In the street the sword will make them childless; in their homes terror will reign. The young men and young women will perish, the infants and those with gray hair. **I said I would scatter them and erase their name from human memory, but I dreaded the taunt of the enemy, lest the adversary misunderstand and say, 'Our hand has triumphed; the LORD has not done all this.**'" They are a nation without sense, there is no discernment in them. If only they were wise and would understand this and discern what their end will be! How could one man chase a thousand, or two put ten thousand to flight, unless their Rock had sold them, unless the LORD had given them up? For their rock is not like our Rock, as even our enemies concede. Their vine comes from the vine of Sodom and from the fields of Gomorrah. Their grapes are filled with poison, and their clusters with bitterness. Their wine is the venom of serpents, the deadly poison of cobras. "Have I not kept this in reserve and sealed it in my vaults? It is mine to avenge; I will repay. In due time their foot will slip; their day of disaster is near and their doom rushes upon them." **The LORD will vindicate his people and relent concerning his servants when he sees their strength is gone and no one is left, slave or free.** He will say: "Now where are their gods, the rock they took refuge in, the gods who ate the fat of their sacrifices and drank the wine of their drink offerings? Let them rise up to help you! Let them give you shelter! "See now that I myself am he! There is no god besides me. I put to death and I bring to life, I have wounded and I will heal, and no one can deliver out of my hand. I lift my hand to heaven and solemnly swear: As surely as I live forever, when I sharpen my flashing sword and my hand grasps it in judgment, I will take vengeance on my adversaries and repay those who hate me. I will make my arrows drunk with blood, while my sword devours flesh: the blood of the slain and the captives, the heads of the enemy leaders." **Rejoice, you nations, with his people, for he will avenge the blood of his servants; he will take vengeance on his enemies and make atonement for his land and people**.

Isaiah 45:17-25: But **Israel will be saved by the LORD with an everlasting salvation; you will never be put to shame or disgraced, to ages everlasting.** For this is what the LORD says – he who created the heavens, he is God; he who fashioned and made the earth, he founded it; he did not create it to be empty, but formed it to be inhabited – he says: "I am the LORD, and there is no other. I have not spoken in secret, from somewhere in a land of darkness; I have not said to Jacob's descendants, 'Seek me in vain.' I, the LORD, speak the truth; I declare what is right. "Gather together and come; assemble, you fugitives from the nations. Ignorant are those who carry about idols of wood, who pray to gods that cannot save. Declare what is to be, present it – let them take counsel together. Who foretold this long ago, who declared it from the distant past? Was it not I, the LORD? And there is no God apart from me, a righteous God and a Savior; there is none but me. "**Turn to me and be saved, all you ends of the earth; for I am God, and there is no other**. By myself I have sworn, my mouth has uttered in all integrity a word that will not be revoked: Before me every knee will bow; by me every tongue will swear. They will say of me, 'In the LORD alone are deliverance and strength.'" All who have raged against him will come to him and be

The Third Day (Tuesday): The Nations & the Day of the Lord

put to shame. **But all the descendants of Israel will find deliverance in the LORD and will make their boast in him.**

Ezekiel 36:24-36: For I will take you out of the nations; **I will gather you from all the countries and bring you back into your own land.** I will sprinkle clean water on you, and you will be clean; **I will cleanse you from all your impurities** and from all your idols. **I will give you a new heart and put a new spirit in you**; I will remove from you your heart of stone and give you a heart of flesh. And I will put my Spirit in you and move you to follow my decrees and be careful to keep my laws. **Then you will live in the land I gave your ancestors; you will be my people, and I will be your God. I will save you from all your uncleanness**. I will call for the grain and make it plentiful and will not bring famine upon you. I will increase the fruit of the trees and the crops of the field, so that you will no longer suffer disgrace among the nations because of famine. Then you will remember your evil ways and wicked deeds, and you will loathe yourselves for your sins and detestable practices. I want you to know that I am not doing this for your sake, declares the Sovereign LORD. Be ashamed and disgraced for your conduct, people of Israel!" 'This is what the Sovereign LORD says: **On the day I cleanse you from all your sins, I will resettle your towns, and the ruins will be rebuilt**. The desolate land will be cultivated instead of lying desolate in the sight of all who pass through it. They will say, "This land that was laid waste has become like the garden of Eden; the cities that were lying in ruins, desolate and destroyed, are now fortified and inhabited." Then the nations around you that remain will know that I the LORD have rebuilt what was destroyed and have replanted what was desolate. I the LORD have spoken, and I will do it.'

Zephaniah 3:11-20: "On that day you, **Jerusalem**, will not be put to shame for all the wrongs you have done to me, because I will remove from you your arrogant boasters. Never again will you be haughty on my holy hill. But I will leave within you the meek and humble. **The remnant of Israel will trust in the name of the LORD.** They will do no wrong; they will tell no lies. A deceitful tongue will not be found in their mouths. They will eat and lie down and no one will make them afraid. Sing, Daughter Zion; shout aloud, Israel! Be glad and rejoice with all your heart, Daughter Jerusalem! The LORD has taken away your punishment, he has turned back your enemy. **The LORD, the King of Israel, is with you; never again will you fear any harm.** On that day they will say to Jerusalem, "Do not fear, Zion; do not let your hands hang limp. The LORD your God is with you, the Mighty Warrior who saves. He will take great delight in you; in his love he will no longer rebuke you, but will rejoice over you with singing." I will remove from you all who mourn over the loss of your appointed festivals, which is a burden and reproach for you. At that time I will deal with all who oppressed you. I will rescue the lame; I will gather the exiles. I will give them praise and honor in every land where they have suffered shame. **At that time I will gather you; at that time I will bring you home.** I will give you honor and praise among all the peoples of the earth when I restore your fortunes before your very eyes," says the LORD.

Deuteronomy 4:26-31: I call the heavens and the earth as witnesses against you this day that you will quickly perish from the land that you are crossing the Jordan to possess. You will not live there long but will certainly be destroyed. **The LORD will scatter you among the peoples, and only a few of you will survive among the nations to which the LORD will drive**

you. There you will worship man-made gods of wood and stone, which cannot see or hear or eat or smell. **But if from there you seek the LORD your God, you will find him if you seek him with all your heart and with all your soul.** When you are in distress and all these things have happened to you, then **in later days you will return to the LORD your God and obey him.** For the LORD your God is a merciful God; he will not abandon or destroy you or forget the covenant with your ancestors, which he confirmed to them by oath.

Deuteronomy 30:1-10: When all these blessings and curses I have set before you come on you **and you take them to heart wherever the LORD your God disperses you among the nations**, and when you and your children return to the LORD your God and obey him with all your heart and with all your soul according to everything I command you today, then the LORD your God will restore your fortunes and have compassion on you and **gather you again from all the nations where he scattered you. Even if you have been banished to the most distant land under the heavens, from there the LORD your God will gather you and bring you back.** He will bring you to the land that belonged to your ancestors, and you will take possession of it. He will make you more prosperous and numerous than your ancestors. **The LORD your God will circumcise your hearts** and the hearts of your descendants, so that you may love him with all your heart and with all your soul, and live. The LORD your God will put all these curses on your enemies who hate and persecute you. You will again obey the LORD and follow all his commands I am giving you today. Then the LORD your God will make you most prosperous in all the work of your hands and in the fruit of your womb, the young of your livestock and the crops of your land. **The LORD will again delight in you and make you prosperous**, just as he delighted in your ancestors, if you obey the LORD your God and keep his commands and decrees that are written in this Book of the Law and turn to the LORD your God with all your heart and with all your soul.

Jeremiah 16:14-16: "However, the days are coming," declares the LORD, "when it will no longer be said, 'As surely as the LORD lives, who brought the Israelites up out of Egypt,' but it will be said, 'As surely as the LORD lives, **who brought the Israelites up out of the land of the north and out of all the countries where he had banished them.**' For I will restore them to the land I gave their ancestors. "But now I will send for many fishermen," declares the LORD, "and they will catch them. After that I will send for many hunters, and they will hunt them down on every mountain and hill and from the crevices of the rocks.

Zechariah 8:7-8: This is what the LORD Almighty says: "**I will save my people from the countries of the east and the west.** I will bring them back to live in Jerusalem; they will be my people, and I will be faithful and righteous to them as their God."

Amos 9:13-15: "The days are coming," declares the LORD, "when the reaper will be overtaken by the plowman and the planter by the one treading grapes. New wine will drip from the mountains and flow from all the hills, and **I will bring my people Israel back from exile.** "They will rebuild the ruined cities and live in them. They will plant vineyards and drink their wine; they will make gardens and eat their fruit. **I will plant Israel in their own land, never again to be uprooted from the land I have given them,**" says the LORD your God.

The Third Day (Tuesday): The Nations & the Day of the Lord

Isaiah 43:4-7: **Since you are precious and honored in my sight, and because I love you**, I will give people in exchange for you, nations in exchange for your life. Do not be afraid, for I am with you; **I will bring your children from the east and gather you from the west.** I will say to the north, 'Give them up!' and to the south, 'Do not hold them back.' **Bring my sons from afar and my daughters from the ends of the earth**-- everyone who is called by my name, whom I created for my glory, whom I formed and made."

Jeremiah 23:3-4: - "I myself will **gather the remnant of my flock** out of all the countries where I have driven them and will bring them back to their pasture, where they will be fruitful and increase in number. I will place shepherds over them who will tend them, and they will no longer be afraid or terrified, **nor will any be missing**," declares the LORD.

Jacob's Trouble:
Jeremiah 30:3-24: The days are coming,' declares the LORD, 'when **I will bring my people Israel and Judah back from captivity and restore them to the land I gave their ancestors to possess,**' says the LORD. These are the words the LORD spoke concerning Israel and Judah: "This is what the LORD says: " **'Cries of fear are heard--terror, not peace**. Ask and see: Can a man bear children? Then why do I see every strong man with his hands on his stomach like a woman in labor, every face turned deathly pale? How awful that day will be! No other will be like it. **It will be a time of trouble for Jacob, but he will be saved out of it.** " 'In that day,' declares the LORD Almighty, 'I will break the yoke off their necks and will tear off their bonds; no longer will foreigners enslave them. Instead, they will serve the LORD their God and David their king, whom I will raise up for them. "So do not be afraid, Jacob my servant; do not be dismayed, Israel,' declares the LORD. **'I will surely save you out of a distant place, your descendants from the land of their exile. Jacob will again have peace and security, and no one will make him afraid.** I am with you and will save you,' declares the LORD. 'Though I completely destroy all the nations among which I scatter you, I will not completely destroy you. **I will discipline you but only in due measure; I will not let you go entirely unpunished**. This is what the LORD says: " 'Your wound is incurable, your injury beyond healing. There is no one to plead your cause, no remedy for your sore, no healing for you. **All your allies have forgotten you; they care nothing for you.** I have struck you as an enemy would and punished you as would the cruel, because your guilt is so great and your sins so many. Why do you cry out over your wound, your pain that has no cure? Because of your great guilt and many sins I have done these things to you. " 'But all who devour you will be devoured; all your enemies will go into exile. Those who plunder you will be plundered; all who make spoil of you I will despoil. But I will restore you to health and heal your wounds,' declares the LORD, 'because you are called an outcast, Zion for whom no one cares.' "This is what the LORD says: " **'I will restore the fortunes of Jacob's tents and have compassion on his dwellings**; the city will be rebuilt on her ruins, and the palace will stand in its proper place. **From them will come songs of thanksgiving and the sound of rejoicing**. I will add to their numbers, and they will not be decreased; I will bring them honor, and they will not be disdained. Their children will be as in days of old, and their community will be established before me; I will punish all who oppress them. **Their leader will be one of their own; their ruler will arise from among them**. I will bring him near and he will come close to me--for who is he who will devote himself to be close to me?' declares the LORD. "**So you will be my people, and I will be your God.**' " See, the storm of the LORD

will burst out in wrath, a driving wind swirling down on the heads of the wicked. The fierce anger of the LORD will not turn back until he fully accomplishes the purposes of his heart. In days to come you will understand this.

Jeremiah 32:37-41: **I will surely gather them from all the lands where I banish them** in my furious anger and great wrath; I will bring them back to this place and let them live in safety. **They will be my people, and I will be their God.** I will give them singleness of heart and action, so that they will always fear me and that all will then go well for them and for their children after them. I will make an everlasting covenant with them: I will never stop doing good to them, and I will inspire them to fear me, so that they will never turn away from me. I will rejoice in doing them good and will assuredly plant them in this land with all my heart and soul.

Ezekiel 11:14-20: The word of the LORD came to me: "Son of man, the people of Jerusalem have said of your fellow exiles and all the other Israelites, 'They are far away from the LORD; this land was given to us as our possession.' "Therefore say: 'This is what the Sovereign LORD says: Although I sent them far away among the nations and scattered them among the countries, yet for a little while I have been a sanctuary for them in the countries where they have gone.' "Therefore say: 'This is what the Sovereign LORD says: **I will gather you from the nations and bring you back from the countries where you have been scattered, and I will give you back the land of Israel again**.' "They will return to it and remove all its vile images and detestable idols. I will give them an undivided heart and put a new spirit in them; I will remove from them their heart of stone and give them a heart of flesh. Then they will follow my decrees and be careful to keep my laws. They will be my people, and I will be their God.

Ezekiel 20:34-38, 40-44: **I will bring you from the nations and gather you from the countries where you have been scattered**--with a mighty hand and an outstretched arm and with outpoured wrath. I will bring you into the wilderness of the nations and there, face to face, I will execute judgment upon you. As I judged your ancestors in the wilderness of the land of Egypt, so I will judge you, declares the Sovereign LORD. **I will take note of you as you pass under my rod, and I will bring you into the bond of the covenant. I will purge you of those who revolt and rebel against me. Although I will bring them out of the land where they are living, yet they will not enter the land of Israel**. Then you will know that I am the LORD. ... For on my holy mountain, the high mountain of Israel, declares the Sovereign LORD, there in the land all the people of Israel will serve me, and there I will accept them. There I will require your offerings and your choice gifts, along with all your holy sacrifices. **I will accept you as fragrant incense when I bring you out from the nations and gather you from the countries where you have been scattered, and I will be proved holy through you in the sight of the nations**. Then you will know that I am the LORD, **when I bring you into the land of Israel**, the land I had sworn with uplifted hand to give to your ancestors. There you will remember your conduct and all the actions by which you have defiled yourselves, and you will loathe yourselves for all the evil you have done. You will know that I am the LORD, when I deal with you for my name's sake and not according to your evil ways and your corrupt practices, you people of Israel, declares the Sovereign LORD.' "

The Fourth Day (Wednesday)
WISDOM FROM ABOVE

INDEX OF TOPICS:
- Jesus is God's Wisdom
- Wisdom from Above
- The Call, Value, and Blessing of Wisdom
- Scriptures About Wisdom
- Discernment & Discretion
- Ungodly Wisdom & the Vanity of Wisdom

JESUS IS GOD'S WISDOM

1 Corinthians 1:17-31: For Christ did not send me to baptize, but to preach the gospel – **not with wisdom and eloquence**, lest the cross of Christ be emptied of its power. For the message of the cross is foolishness to those who are perishing, but to us who are being saved it is the power of God. For it is written: "I will destroy the wisdom of the wise; the intelligence of the intelligent I will frustrate." Where is the wise person? Where is the teacher of the law? Where is the philosopher of this age? **Has not God made foolish the wisdom of the world?** For since in the **wisdom of God** the world through its wisdom did not know him, God was pleased through the foolishness of what was preached to save those who believe. Jews demand signs and Greeks look for wisdom, but we preach Christ crucified: a stumbling block to Jews and foolishness to Gentiles, but to those whom God has called, both Jews and Greeks, **Christ the power of God and the wisdom of God**. For the foolishness of God is wiser than human wisdom, and the weakness of God is stronger than human strength. Brothers and sisters, think of what you were when you were called. Not many of you were wise by human standards; not many were influential; not many were of noble birth. But God chose the foolish things of the world to shame the wise; God chose the weak things of the world to shame the strong. God chose the lowly things of this world and the despised things – and the things that are not – to nullify the things that are, so that no one may boast before him. **It is because of him that you are in Christ Jesus, who has become for us wisdom from God** – that is, our righteousness, holiness and redemption. Therefore, as it is written: "Let the one who boasts boast in the Lord."

1 Corinthians 2:1-13: And so it was with me, brothers and sisters. When I came to you, **I did not come with eloquence or human wisdom** as I proclaimed to you the testimony about God. For I resolved to know nothing while I was with you except Jesus Christ and him crucified. I came to you in weakness with great fear and trembling. My message and my preaching were **not with wise and persuasive words**, but with a demonstration of the

Spirit's power, **so that your faith might not rest on human wisdom, but on God's power**. We do, however, **speak a message of wisdom among the mature, but not the wisdom of this age or of the rulers of this age**, who are coming to nothing. No, we declare **God's wisdom**, a mystery that has been hidden and that God destined for our glory before time began. None of the rulers of this age understood it, for if they had, they would not have crucified the Lord of glory. However, as it is written: "What no eye has seen, what no ear has heard, and what no human mind has conceived" – the things God has prepared for those who love him – these are the things God has revealed to us by his Spirit. The Spirit searches all things, even the deep things of God. For who knows a person's thoughts except their own spirit within them? In the same way no one knows the thoughts of God except the Spirit of God. What we have received is not the spirit of the world, but the Spirit who is from God, so that we may understand what God has freely given us. This is what we speak, **not in words taught us by human wisdom but in words taught by the Spirit**, explaining spiritual realities with Spirit-taught words.

Matthew 11:16-19: "To what can I compare this generation? They are like children sitting in the marketplaces and calling out to others: " 'We played the pipe for you, and you did not dance; we sang a dirge, and you did not mourn.' For John came neither eating nor drinking, and they say, 'He has a demon.' The Son of Man came eating and drinking, and they say, 'Here is a glutton and a drunkard, a friend of tax collectors and sinners.' **But wisdom is proved right by her deeds**."

Matthew 12:42: The Queen of the South will rise at the judgment with this generation and condemn it; for she came from the ends of the earth to listen to **Solomon's wisdom, and now something greater than Solomon is here**.

Isaiah 11:2-4: **The Spirit of the LORD will rest on him – the Spirit of wisdom and of understanding**, the Spirit of counsel and of might, the Spirit of the knowledge and fear of the LORD – and he will delight in the fear of the LORD. He will not judge by what he sees with his eyes, or decide by what he hears with his ears; but with righteousness he will judge the needy, with justice he will give decisions for the poor of the earth. He will strike the earth with the rod of his mouth; with the breath of his lips he will slay the wicked.

Luke 2:40, 52: And the child [Jesus] grew and became strong; **he was filled with wisdom**, and the grace of God was on him. ... And Jesus **grew in wisdom and stature**, and in favor with God and man.

Revelation 5:12: In a loud voice they were saying: "Worthy is the Lamb, who was slain, to receive power and wealth and **wisdom** and strength and honor and glory and praise!"

Revelation 7:11-12: All the angels were standing around the throne and around the elders and the four living creatures. They fell down on their faces before the throne and worshiped God, saying: "Amen! Praise and glory and **wisdom** and thanks and honor and power and strength be to our God for ever and ever. Amen!"

WISDOM FROM ABOVE

James 1:5-8:- If any of you lacks **wisdom**, you should ask God, who gives generously to all without finding fault, and it will be given to you. But when you ask, you must believe and not doubt, because the one who doubts is like a wave of the sea, blown and tossed by the wind. That person should not expect to receive anything from the Lord. Such a person is double-minded and unstable in all they do.

James 3:13-18: **Who is wise** and understanding among you? Let them show it by their good life, by deeds done in the humility that comes from wisdom. But if you harbor bitter envy and selfish ambition in your hearts, do not boast about it or deny the truth. **Such "wisdom"** does not come down from heaven but is earthly, unspiritual, demonic. For where you have envy and selfish ambition, there you find disorder and every evil practice. **But the wisdom that comes from heaven** is first of all pure; then peace-loving, considerate, submissive, full of mercy and good fruit, impartial and sincere. Peacemakers who sow in peace reap a harvest of righteousness.

Luke 21:13-15: And so you will bear testimony to me. But make up your mind not to worry beforehand how you will defend yourselves. For I will give you words and **wisdom** that none of your adversaries will be able to resist or contradict.

Ephesians 1:17: I keep asking that the God of our Lord Jesus Christ, the glorious Father, may give you the **Spirit of wisdom** and revelation, so that you may know him better.

Colossians 4:5-6: **Be wise** in the way you act toward outsiders; make the most of every opportunity. Let your conversation be always full of grace, seasoned with salt, so that you may know how to answer everyone.

Colossians 1:9: For this reason, since the day we heard about you, we have not stopped praying for you. We continually ask God to fill you with the knowledge of his will through **all the wisdom and understanding that the Spirit gives**,

Ephesians 3:10-11: His intent was that now, through the church, **the manifold wisdom of God** should be made known to the rulers and authorities in the heavenly realms, according to his eternal purpose that he accomplished in Christ Jesus our Lord.

Colossians 1:28: He is the one we proclaim, admonishing and teaching everyone **with all wisdom**, so that we may present everyone fully mature in Christ.

Colossians 2:2-3: My goal is that they may be encouraged in heart and united in love, so that they may have the full riches of complete understanding, in order that they may know the mystery of God, namely, Christ, in whom are hidden **all the treasures of wisdom and knowledge.**

Colossians 2:20-23: Since you died with Christ to the elemental spiritual forces of this world, why, as though you still belonged to the world, do you submit to its rules: "Do not handle!

Do not taste! Do not touch!"? These rules, which have to do with things that are all destined to perish with use, are based on merely human commands and teachings. Such regulations indeed have an **appearance of wisdom**, with their self-imposed worship, their false humility and their harsh treatment of the body, but they lack any value in restraining sensual indulgence.

Colossians 3:16: Let the message of Christ dwell among you richly as you teach and admonish one another with **all wisdom** through psalms, hymns, and songs from the Spirit, singing to God with gratitude in your hearts.

Revelation 13:18: **This calls for wisdom.** Let the person who has insight calculate the number of the beast, for it is the number of a man. That number is 666.

Revelation 17:9-14: "**This calls for a mind with wisdom.** The seven heads are seven hills on which the woman sits. They are also seven kings. Five have fallen, one is, the other has not yet come; but when he does come, he must remain for only a little while. The beast who once was, and now is not, is an eighth king. He belongs to the seven and is going to his destruction. "The ten horns you saw are ten kings who have not yet received a kingdom, but who for one hour will receive authority as kings along with the beast. They have one purpose and will give their power and authority to the beast. They will wage war against the Lamb, but the Lamb will triumph over them because he is Lord of lords and King of kings – and with him will be his called, chosen and faithful followers."

THE CALL, VALUE, AND BLESSING OF WISDOM

Proverbs 1:20-33: [The Call of Wisdom] Out in the open **wisdom calls aloud**, she raises her voice in the public square; on top of the wall she cries out, at the city gate **she makes her speech**: "How long will you who are simple love your simple ways? How long will mockers delight in mockery and fools hate knowledge? Repent at my rebuke! Then I will pour out my thoughts to you, I will make known to you my teachings. But since you refuse to listen when I call and no one pays attention when I stretch out my hand, since you disregard all my advice and do not accept my rebuke, I in turn will laugh when disaster strikes you; I will mock when calamity overtakes you – when calamity overtakes you like a storm, when disaster sweeps over you like a whirlwind, when distress and trouble overwhelm you. Then they will call to me but I will not answer; they will look for me but will not find me, since they hated knowledge and did not choose to fear the LORD. Since they would not accept my advice and spurned my rebuke, they will eat the fruit of their ways and be filled with the fruit of their schemes. For the waywardness of the simple will kill them, and the complacency of fools will destroy them; but whoever listens to me will live in safety and be at ease, without fear of harm."

Proverbs 8:1-21: **Does not wisdom call out?** Does not understanding raise her voice? At the highest point along the way, where the paths meet, she takes her stand; beside the gate leading into the city, at the entrance, **she cries aloud**: "To you, O people, I call out; I raise my voice to all mankind. You who are simple, gain prudence; you who are foolish, set your

The Fourth Day (Wednesday): Wisdom from Above

hearts on it. Listen, for I have trustworthy things to say; I open my lips to speak what is right. **My mouth speaks what is true**, for my lips detest wickedness. All the words of my mouth are just; none of them is crooked or perverse. To the discerning all of them are right; they are upright to those who have found knowledge. **Choose my instruction instead of silver, knowledge rather than choice gold, for wisdom is more precious than rubies, and nothing you desire can compare with her.** "I, wisdom, dwell together with prudence; I possess knowledge and discretion. To fear the LORD is to hate evil; I hate pride and arrogance, evil behavior and perverse speech. Counsel and sound judgment are mine; I have insight, I have power. By me kings reign and rulers issue decrees that are just; by me princes govern, and nobles – all who rule on earth. I love those who love me, and those who seek me find me. With me are riches and honor, enduring wealth and prosperity. **My fruit is better than fine gold; what I yield surpasses choice silver**. I walk in the way of righteousness, along the paths of justice, bestowing a rich inheritance on those who love me and making their treasuries full."

Proverbs 8:32-36: "Now then, my children, **listen to me [wisdom]; blessed are those who keep my ways. Listen to my instruction and be wise**; do not disregard it. Blessed are those who listen to me, watching daily at my doors, waiting at my doorway. For **those who find me find life and receive favor from the LORD**. But those who fail to find me harm themselves; all who hate me love death."

Proverbs 2:1-22: [The Value of Wisdom] My son, if you accept my words and store up my commands within you, **turning your ear to wisdom** and applying your heart to understanding – indeed, if you call out for insight and cry aloud for understanding, and if you look for it as for silver and search for it as for hidden treasure, then you will understand the fear of the LORD and find the knowledge of God. **For the LORD gives wisdom**; from his mouth come knowledge and understanding. **He holds success in store for the upright**, he is a shield to those whose walk is blameless, for he guards the course of the just and protects the way of his faithful ones. Then you will understand what is right and just and fair – every good path. **For wisdom will enter your heart**, and knowledge will be pleasant to your soul. **Discretion will protect you**, and **understanding will guard you. Wisdom will save you** from the ways of wicked men, from men whose words are perverse, who have left the straight paths to walk in dark ways, who delight in doing wrong and rejoice in the perverseness of evil, whose paths are crooked and who are devious in their ways. **Wisdom will save you** also from the adulterous woman, from the wayward woman with her seductive words, who has left the partner of her youth and ignored the covenant she made before God. Surely her house leads down to death and her paths to the spirits of the dead. None who go to her return or attain the paths of life. **Thus you will walk in the ways of the good and keep to the paths of the righteous**. For the upright will live in the land, and the blameless will remain in it; but the wicked will be cut off from the land, and the unfaithful will be torn from it.

Proverbs 3:13-18: [The Blessing of Wisdom] **Blessed are those who find wisdom**, those who gain understanding, **for she is more profitable than silver and yields better returns than gold. She is more precious than rubies; nothing you desire can compare with her.** Long life is in her right hand; in her left hand are riches and honor. Her ways are pleasant ways, and all her paths are peace. **She is a tree of life to those who take hold of her**; those who hold her fast will be blessed.

Proverbs 4:5-9: **Get wisdom**, get understanding; do not forget my words or turn away from them. **Do not forsake wisdom**, and she will protect you; love her, and she will watch over you. **The beginning of wisdom is this: Get wisdom.** Though it cost all you have, get understanding. Cherish her, and she will exalt you; embrace her, and she will honor you. She will give you a garland to grace your head and present you with a glorious crown."

SCRIPTURES ABOUT WISDOM

Psalm 111:10: **The fear of the LORD is the beginning of wisdom**; all who follow his precepts have good understanding. To him belongs eternal praise.

Deuteronomy 4:6: Observe them [God's commands] carefully, for this will show your wisdom and understanding to the nations, who will hear about all these decrees and say, "Surely this great nation is a **wise and understanding** people."

Isaiah 33:5-6: The LORD is exalted, for he dwells on high; he will fill Zion with his justice and righteousness. He will be the sure foundation for your times, **a rich store of salvation and wisdom and knowledge**; the fear of the LORD is the key to this treasure.

Hosea 14:9: **Who is wise?** Let them realize these things. Who is discerning? Let them understand. The ways of the LORD are right; the righteous walk in them, but the rebellious stumble in them.

Psalm 19:7: The law of the LORD is perfect, refreshing the soul. The statutes of the LORD are trustworthy, **making wise the simple.**

Psalm 37:30: **The mouths of the righteous utter wisdom**, and their tongues speak what is just.

Psalm 49:3: My mouth will speak **words of wisdom**; the meditation of my heart will give you understanding.

Psalm 51:6: Yet you desired faithfulness even in the womb; **you taught me wisdom** in that secret place.

Psalm 90:12: Teach us to number our days, that we may **gain a heart of wisdom.**

Psalm 119:98: Your commands are always with me and make me **wiser than my enemies.**

Proverbs 9:10-12: **The fear of the LORD is the beginning of wisdom**, and knowledge of the Holy One is understanding. For through wisdom your days will be many, and years will be

The Fourth Day (Wednesday): Wisdom from Above

added to your life. **If you are wise**, your wisdom will reward you; if you are a mocker, you alone will suffer.

Proverbs 6:6-8: Go to the ant, you sluggard; consider its ways and **be wise!** It has no commander, no overseer or ruler, yet it stores its provisions in summer and gathers its food at harvest.

Proverbs 7:4-5: **Say to wisdom**, "You are my sister," and to insight, "You are my relative." They will keep you from the adulterous woman, from the wayward woman with her seductive words.

Proverbs 10:13-14: **Wisdom is found on the lips of the discerning**, but a rod is for the back of one who has no sense. **The wise** store up knowledge, but the mouth of a fool invites ruin.

Proverbs 10:31: From the mouth of the righteous comes the **fruit of wisdom**, but a perverse tongue will be silenced.

Proverbs 11:2: When pride comes, then comes disgrace, but with **humility comes wisdom**.

Proverbs 13:10: Where there is strife, there is pride, but **wisdom is found** in those who take advice.

Proverbs 13:20: **Walk with the wise and become wise**, for a companion of fools suffers harm.

Proverbs 14:6-8: The mocker seeks wisdom and finds none, but knowledge comes easily to the discerning. Stay away from a fool, for you will not find knowledge on their lips. **The wisdom of the prudent** is to give thought to their ways, but the folly of fools is deception.

Proverbs 14:33: **Wisdom reposes** in the heart of the discerning and even among fools she lets herself be known.

Proverbs 15:33: **Wisdom's instruction is to fear the LORD**, and humility comes before honor.

Proverbs 16:16: How much better to get **wisdom** than gold, to get insight rather than silver!

Proverbs 17:24: **A discerning person keeps wisdom in view**, but a fool's eyes wander to the ends of the earth.

Proverbs 18:4: The words of the mouth are deep waters, but the **fountain of wisdom** is a rushing stream.

Proverbs 19:11: A person's **wisdom yields patience**; it is to one's glory to overlook an offense.

Proverbs 19:20: Listen to advice and accept discipline, and at the end you will be **counted among the wise**.

Proverbs 20:1: Wine is a mocker and beer a brawler; whoever is led astray by them is **not wise**.

Proverbs 21:11: When a mocker is punished, the **simple gain wisdom**; by paying attention to the wise they get knowledge.

Proverbs 21:30-31: **There is no wisdom**, no insight, no plan that can succeed against the LORD. The horse is made ready for the day of battle, but victory rests with the LORD.

Proverbs 23:15-18: My son, **if your heart is wise**, then my heart will be glad indeed; my inmost being will rejoice when your lips speak what is right. Do not let your heart envy sinners, but always be zealous for the fear of the LORD. There is surely a future hope for you, and your hope will not be cut off.

Proverbs 23-24: Buy the truth and do not sell it – **wisdom**, instruction and insight as well. The father of a righteous child has great joy; a man who fathers **a wise son** rejoices in him.

Proverbs 24:7: **Wisdom** is too high for fools; in the assembly at the gate they must not open their mouths.

Proverbs 24:14: **Know also that wisdom is like honey for you**: If you find it, there is a future hope for you, and your hope will not be cut off.

Proverbs 28:26: Those who trust in themselves are fools, but those who **walk in wisdom** are kept safe.

Proverbs 29:15: **A rod and a reprimand impart wisdom**, but a child left undisciplined disgraces its mother.

Proverbs 30:24-28: "Four things on earth are small, yet they are **extremely wise**: Ants are creatures of little strength, yet they store up their food in the summer; hyraxes are creatures of little power, yet they make their home in the crags; locusts have no king, yet they advance together in ranks; a lizard can be caught with the hand, yet it is found in kings' palaces.

1 Kings 4:29-34: God gave Solomon **wisdom** and very great insight, and a breadth of understanding as measureless as the sand on the seashore. Solomon's **wisdom** was greater than the **wisdom** of all the people of the East, and greater than all the wisdom of Egypt. He was wiser than anyone else, including Ethan the Ezrahite – wiser than Heman, Kalkol and Darda, the sons of Mahol. And his fame spread to all the surrounding nations. He spoke three thousand proverbs and his songs numbered a thousand and five. He spoke about plant life, from the cedar of Lebanon to the hyssop that grows out of walls. He also spoke about animals and birds, reptiles and fish. From all nations people came to listen to Solomon's **wisdom**, sent by all the kings of the world, who had heard of his **wisdom**.

The Fourth Day (Wednesday): Wisdom from Above

Daniel 1:20: In **every matter of wisdom and understanding** about which the king questioned them, he found them [Daniel and his friends] ten times better than all the magicians and enchanters in his whole kingdom.

Proverbs 3:19-24: **By wisdom the LORD laid the earth's foundations**, by understanding he set the heavens in place; by his knowledge the watery depths were divided, and the clouds let drop the dew. My son, **do not let wisdom and understanding out of your sight**, preserve sound judgment and discretion; they will be life for you, an ornament to grace your neck. Then you will go on your way in safety, and your foot will not stumble. When you lie down, you will not be afraid; when you lie down, your sleep will be sweet.

Proverbs 24:3-4: **By wisdom a house is built**, and through understanding it is established; through knowledge its rooms are filled with rare and beautiful treasures.

Proverbs 8:22-31: "**The LORD brought me [wisdom] forth** as the first of his works, before his deeds of old; I was formed long ages ago, at the very beginning, when the world came to be. When there were no watery depths, I was given birth, when there were no springs overflowing with water; before the mountains were settled in place, before the hills, I was given birth, before he made the world or its fields or any of the dust of the earth. I was there when he set the heavens in place, when he marked out the horizon on the face of the deep, when he established the clouds above and fixed securely the fountains of the deep, when he gave the sea its boundary so the waters would not overstep his command, and when he marked out the foundations of the earth. Then I was constantly at his side. I was filled with delight day after day, rejoicing always in his presence, rejoicing in his whole world and delighting in mankind.

Ecclesiastes 8:1: **Who is like the wise?** Who knows the explanation of things? A person's wisdom brightens their face and changes its hard appearance.

DISCERNMENT AND DISCRETION

Philippians 1:9-11: And this is my prayer: that your love may abound more and more in knowledge and **depth of insight**, so that you may be able to discern what is best and may be pure and blameless for the day of Christ, filled with the fruit of righteousness that comes through Jesus Christ – to the glory and praise of God.

Hebrews 5:13-14: For everyone who partakes [only] of milk is not accustomed to the word of righteousness, for he is an infant. But solid food is for the mature, who because of practice have their senses trained to **discern good and evil**.

Matthew 16:2-3:- But He replied to them, "When it is evening, you say, 'It will be fair weather, for the sky is red.' "And in the morning, 'There will be a storm today, for the sky is red and threatening.' Do you know how to **discern** the appearance of the sky, **but cannot [discern]** the signs of the times?

Romans 12:2: Do not be conformed to this world, but be transformed by the renewal of your mind, that **by testing you may discern** what is the will of God, what is good and acceptable and perfect.

1 Thessalonians 5:19-22: Do not quench the Spirit. Do not treat prophecies with contempt but **test them all**; hold on to what is good, reject every kind of evil.

1 Corinthians 6:4-5: Therefore, if you have disputes about such matters, do you ask for a ruling from those whose way of life is scorned in the church? I say this to shame you. Is it possible that there is nobody among you **wise enough to judge** a dispute between believers?

Job 12:11: Does not **the ear test words** as the tongue tastes food?

1 Kings 3:8-14: [Solomon's prayer and God's response] Your servant is here among the people you have chosen, a great people, too numerous to count or number. **So give your servant a discerning heart** to govern your people and to distinguish between right and wrong. For who is able to govern this great people of yours?" The Lord was pleased that Solomon had asked for this. So God said to him, "Since you have asked for this and not for long life or wealth for yourself, nor have asked for the death of your enemies but for **discernment** in administering justice, I will do what you have asked. **I will give you a wise and discerning heart**, so that there will never have been anyone like you, nor will there ever be. Moreover, I will give you what you have not asked for – both wealth and honor – so that in your lifetime you will have no equal among kings. And if you walk in obedience to me and keep my decrees and commands as David your father did, I will give you a long life."

From Psalm 119:
v.27: **Cause me to understand** the way of your precepts, that I may meditate on your wonderful deeds.
v.34: **Give me understanding**, so that I may keep your law and obey it with all my heart.
v.73: Your hands made me and formed me; **give me understanding** to learn your commands.
v.100: I have **more understanding** than the elders, for I obey your precepts.
v.104: I **gain understanding** from your precepts; therefore I hate every wrong path.
v.125: I am your servant; **give me discernment** that I may understand your statutes.
v.130: The unfolding of your words gives light; it **gives understanding** to the simple.
v.144: Your statutes are always righteous; **give me understanding** that I may live.
v.169: May my cry come before you, LORD; **give me understanding** according to your word.

UNGODLY WISDOM AND THE VANITY OF WISDOM

James 3:14-16: But if you harbor bitter envy and selfish ambition in your hearts, do not boast about it or deny the truth. **Such "wisdom" does not come down from heaven but is earthly, unspiritual, demonic.** For where you have envy and selfish ambition, there you find disorder and every evil practice.

The Fourth Day (Wednesday): Wisdom from Above

2 Corinthians 1:12: Now this is our boast: Our conscience testifies that we have conducted ourselves in the world, and especially in our relations with you, with integrity and godly sincerity. We have done so, relying **not on worldly wisdom** but on God's grace.

1 Corinthians 3:18-20: Do not deceive yourselves. **If any of you think you are wise by the standards of this age, you should become "fools" so that you may become wise.** For the wisdom of this world is foolishness in God's sight. As it is written: "**He catches the wise in their craftiness**"; and again, "The Lord knows that the thoughts of the wise are futile."

Isaiah 47:8-11: "Now then, listen, [Babylon] you lover of pleasure, lounging in your security and saying to yourself, 'I am, and there is none besides me. I will never be a widow or suffer the loss of children.' Both of these will overtake you in a moment, on a single day: loss of children and widowhood. They will come upon you in full measure, in spite of your many sorceries and all your potent spells. You have trusted in your wickedness and have said, 'No one sees me.' **Your wisdom and knowledge mislead you when you say to yourself, 'I am, and there is none besides me**.' Disaster will come upon you, and you will not know how to conjure it away. A calamity will fall upon you that you cannot ward off with a ransom; a catastrophe you cannot foresee will suddenly come upon you.

Jeremiah 8:7-9: Even the stork in the sky knows her appointed seasons, and the dove, the swift and the thrush observe the time of their migration. But my people do not know the requirements of the LORD. **'How can you say, "We are wise, for we have the law of the LORD**," when actually the lying pen of the scribes has handled it falsely? **The wise will be put to shame**; they will be dismayed and trapped. Since they have rejected the word of the LORD, **what kind of wisdom do they have?**

Jeremiah 9:23-24: This is what the LORD says: "**Let not the wise boast of their wisdom** or the strong boast of their strength or the rich boast of their riches, but let the one who boasts boast about this: that they have the understanding to know me, that I am the LORD, who exercises kindness, justice and righteousness on earth, for in these I delight," declares the LORD.

Ecclesiastes 10:1: As dead flies give perfume a bad smell, **so a little folly outweighs wisdom** and honor.

Ecclesiastes 1:16-18: I said to myself, "Look, I have **increased in wisdom** more than anyone who has ruled over Jerusalem before me; I have experienced much of wisdom and knowledge." Then I applied myself to the **understanding of wisdom**, and also of madness and folly, but I learned that this, too, is a chasing after the wind. For **with much wisdom comes much sorrow**; the more knowledge, the more grief.

Ecclesiastes 2:13-16: I saw that **wisdom is better than folly**, just as light is better than darkness. **The wise have eyes in their heads**, while the fool walks in the darkness; but I came to realize that the same fate overtakes them both. Then I said to myself, "The fate of the fool will overtake me also. What then do I gain by being wise?" I said to myself, "This too is meaningless." For **the wise**, like the fool, will not be long remembered; the days have already come when both have been forgotten. Like the fool, **the wise** too must die!

Ecclesiastes 2:26: **To the person who pleases him, God gives wisdom**, knowledge and happiness, but to the sinner he gives the task of gathering and storing up wealth to hand it over to the one who pleases God. This too is meaningless, a chasing after the wind.

Ecclesiastes 9:11: I have seen something else under the sun: The race is not to the swift or the battle to the strong, nor does food come to **the wise** or wealth to the brilliant or favor to the learned; but time and chance happen to them all.

Ecclesiastes 9:13-18: I also saw under the sun **this example of wisdom** that greatly impressed me: There was once a small city with only a few people in it. And a powerful king came against it, surrounded it and built huge siege works against it. Now there lived in that city **a man poor but wise, and he saved the city by his wisdom**. But nobody remembered that poor man. So I said, "**Wisdom is better than strength.**" **But the poor man's wisdom is despised**, and his words are no longer heeded. The quiet **words of the wise** are more to be heeded than the shouts of a ruler of fools. **Wisdom is better than weapons of war**, but one sinner destroys much good.

The Fifth Day (Thursday)
THE PERSECUTED, POOR & OPPRESSED

INDEX OF TOPICS:
- The Persecuted (for their faith in Christ)
- The Imprisoned
- The Poor & Needy, Widows and Fatherless/Orphans
- The Sick (Oppressed by the Devil)

Isaiah 61:1-3: The Spirit of the Sovereign LORD is on me, because the LORD has anointed me to **proclaim good news to the poor**. He has sent me to bind up the brokenhearted, to proclaim **freedom for the captives and release from darkness for the prisoners**, to proclaim the year of the LORD's favor and the day of vengeance of our God, to comfort all who mourn, and provide for those who grieve in Zion--to bestow on them a crown of beauty instead of ashes, the oil of joy instead of mourning, and a garment of praise instead of a spirit of despair. They will be called oaks of righteousness, a planting of the LORD for the display of his splendor.

THE PERSECUTED

Psalms List for those Being Persecuted

Psalm 7	Psalm 23	Psalm 35	Psalm 70	Psalm 88	Psalm 109
Psalm 10	Psalm 27	Psalm 37	Psalm 71	Psalm 91	Psalm 142
Psalm 22	Psalm 31	Psalm 68	Psalm 73	Psalm 94	Psalm 143

2 Timothy 3:12-13: In fact, **everyone who wants to live a godly life in Christ Jesus will be persecuted**, while evildoers and impostors will go from bad to worse, deceiving and being deceived.

Revelation 13:1-10: The dragon stood on the shore of the sea. And I saw a beast coming out of the sea. It had ten horns and seven heads, with ten crowns on its horns, and on each head a blasphemous name. The beast I saw resembled a leopard, but had feet like those of a bear and a mouth like that of a lion. The dragon gave the beast his power and his throne and great authority. One of the heads of the beast seemed to have had a fatal wound, but the fatal wound had been healed. The whole world was filled with wonder and followed the beast. People worshiped the dragon because he had given authority to the beast, and they also worshiped the beast and asked, "Who is like the beast? Who can wage war against it?" The beast was given a mouth to utter proud words and blasphemies and to exercise its authority for forty-two months. It opened its mouth to blaspheme God, and to slander his name and his dwelling place and those who live in heaven. **It was given power to wage war against God's holy people and to conquer them.** And it was given authority over every tribe, people, language and nation. All inhabitants of the earth will worship the beast--all whose names have not been written in the Lamb's book of life, the Lamb who was slain from the creation of the world. **Whoever has ears, let them hear. "If anyone is to go into captivity, into captivity they will go. If anyone is to be killed with the sword, with the sword they will be killed." This calls for patient endurance and faithfulness on the part of God's people.**

Romans 8:35-39: Who shall separate us from the love of Christ? Shall **trouble or hardship or persecution** or famine or nakedness or danger or sword? As it is written: "For your sake we face death all day long; we are considered as **sheep to be slaughtered." No, in all these things we are more than conquerors through him who loved us.** For I am convinced that neither death nor life, neither angels nor demons, neither the present nor the future, nor any powers, neither height nor depth, nor anything else in all creation, will be able to separate us from the love of God that is in Christ Jesus our Lord.

Romans 5:3-5: Not only so, but we also **glory in our sufferings**, because we know that suffering produces perseverance; perseverance, character; and character, hope. And hope does not put us to shame, because God's love has been poured out into our hearts through the Holy Spirit, who has been given to us.

1 Thessalonians 3:2-8: We sent Timothy, who is our brother and co-worker in God's service in spreading the gospel of Christ, to strengthen and encourage you in your faith, **so that no one would be unsettled by these trials. For you know quite well that we are destined for them.** In fact, when we were with you, we kept telling you that **we would be persecuted.** And it turned out that way, as you well know. For this reason, when I could stand it no longer, I sent to find out about your faith. I was afraid that in some way the tempter had tempted you and that our labors might have been in vain. But Timothy has just now come to us from you and has brought good news about your faith and love. He has told us that you always have pleasant memories of us and that you long to see us, just as we also long to see you. Therefore, brothers and sisters, **in all our distress and persecution** we were encouraged about you because of your faith. For now we really live, since you are standing firm in the Lord.

2 Thessalonians 1:4-12: Therefore, among God's churches we boast about your **perseverance and faith in all the persecutions and trials you are enduring.** All this is evidence that God's judgment is right, and as a result you will be counted worthy of the **kingdom of God, for which you are suffering.** God is just: He will pay back trouble to those who trouble you and give relief to you who are troubled, and to us as well. This will happen when the Lord Jesus is revealed from heaven in blazing fire with his powerful angels. He will punish those who do not know God and do not obey the gospel of our Lord Jesus. They will be punished with everlasting destruction and shut out from the presence of the

The Fifth Day (Thursday): The Persecuted, Poor, & Oppressed

Lord and from the glory of his might on the day he comes to be glorified in his holy people and to be marveled at among all those who have believed. This includes you, because you believed our testimony to you. With this in mind, we constantly pray for you, that our God may make you worthy of his calling, and that by his power he may bring to fruition your every desire for goodness and your every deed prompted by faith. We pray this so that the name of our Lord Jesus may be glorified in you, and you in him, according to the grace of our God and the Lord Jesus Christ.

Hebrews 10:33-39: Sometimes you were **publicly exposed to insult and persecution**; at other times you stood side by side with those who were so treated. **You suffered along with those in prison and joyfully accepted the confiscation of your property**, because you knew that you yourselves had better and lasting possessions. So do not throw away your confidence; it will be richly rewarded. You need to persevere so that when you have done the will of God, you will receive what he has promised. For, "In just a little while, he who is coming will come and will not delay." And, "But my righteous one will live by faith. And I take no pleasure in the one who shrinks back." But we do not belong to those who shrink back and are destroyed, but to those who have faith and are saved.

1 Peter 2:13-23: Submit yourselves for the Lord's sake to every human authority: whether to the emperor, as the supreme authority, or to governors, who are sent by him to punish those who do wrong and to commend those who do right. For it is God's will that by doing good you should silence the ignorant talk of foolish people. Live as free people, but do not use your freedom as a cover-up for evil; live as God's slaves. Show proper respect to everyone, love the family of believers, fear God, honor the emperor. Slaves, in reverent fear of God submit yourselves to your masters, not only to those who are good and considerate, but also to those who are harsh. **For it is commendable if someone bears up under the pain of unjust suffering because they are conscious of God**. But how is it to your credit if you receive a beating for doing wrong and endure it? **But if you suffer for doing good and you endure it, this is commendable before God. To this you were called, because Christ suffered for you, leaving you an example**, that you should follow in his steps. "He committed no sin, and no deceit was found in his mouth." When they hurled their insults at him, he did not retaliate; when he suffered, he made no threats. Instead, he entrusted himself to him who judges justly.

Matthew 13:21: But since they have no root, they last only a short time. **When trouble or persecution comes because of the word**, they quickly fall away.

Matthew 5:10-12: **Blessed are those who are persecuted because of righteousness**, for theirs is the kingdom of heaven. "**Blessed are you when people insult you, persecute you and falsely say all kinds of evil against you because of me**. Rejoice and be glad, because great is your reward in heaven, for in the same way they **persecuted the prophets who were before you**.

Luke 6:22-23, 26: **Blessed are you when people hate you, when they exclude you and insult you and reject your name as evil, because of the Son of Man**. "Rejoice in that day and leap for joy, because great is your reward in heaven. For that is how their ancestors treated the prophets. ... **Woe to you when everyone speaks well of you**, for that is how their ancestors treated the false prophets.

2 Corinthians 6:3-10: We put no stumbling block in anyone's path, so that our ministry will not be discredited. Rather, as servants of God we commend ourselves in every way: in great endurance; **in troubles, hardships and distresses; in beatings, imprisonments and riots; in hard work, sleepless nights and hunger**; in purity, understanding, patience and kindness; in the Holy Spirit and in sincere love; in truthful speech and in the power of God; with weapons of righteousness in the right hand and in the left; through glory and **dishonor, bad report** and good report; genuine, yet **regarded as impostors**; known, yet **regarded as unknown**; **dying**, and yet we live on; **beaten**, and yet not killed; **sorrowful**, yet always rejoicing; **poor**, yet making many rich; **having nothing**, and yet possessing everything.

Matthew 10:23: When you are **persecuted** in one place, flee to another. Truly I tell you, you will not finish going through the towns of Israel before the Son of Man comes.

Luke 21:12: "But before all this, **they will seize you and persecute you**. They will hand you over to synagogues and **put you in prison**, and you will be brought before kings and governors, and all on account of my name.

John 15:20: Remember what I told you: 'A servant is not greater than his master.' **If they persecuted me, they will persecute you also**. If they obeyed my teaching, they will obey yours also.

John 16:33: "I have told you these things, so that in me you may have peace. **In this world you will have trouble**. But take heart! I have overcome the world."

Acts 7:52: Was there ever a prophet your ancestors did not **persecute**? They even killed those who predicted the coming of the Righteous One. And now you have betrayed and murdered him--

Acts 13:50: But the Jewish leaders incited the God-fearing women of high standing and the leading men of the city. They **stirred up persecution** against Paul and Barnabas, and expelled them from their region.

Acts 14:22: strengthening the disciples and encouraging them to remain true to the faith. "**We must go through many hardships to enter the kingdom of God**," they said.

2 Corinthians 12:10: That is why, for Christ's sake, **I delight in weaknesses, in insults, in hardships, in persecutions, in difficulties**. For when I am weak, then I am strong.

2 Timothy 3:10-11: You, however, know all about my teaching, my way of life, my purpose, faith, patience, love, **endurance, persecutions, sufferings**--what kinds of things happened to me in Antioch, Iconium and Lystra, **the persecutions I endured**. Yet the Lord rescued me from all of them.

The Fifth Day (Thursday): The Persecuted, Poor, & Oppressed

Romans 12:12-14: Be joyful in hope, **patient in affliction**, faithful in prayer. Share with the Lord's people who are in need. Practice hospitality. **Bless those who persecute you; bless and do not curse.**

Matthew 5:44: But I tell you, **love your enemies and pray for those who persecute you**,

1 Corinthians 4:12: We work hard with our own hands. **When we are cursed, we bless; when we are persecuted, we endure it**;

2 Corinthians 4:7-12: But we have this treasure in jars of clay to show that this all-surpassing power is from God and not from us. **We are hard pressed on every side**, but not crushed; **perplexed**, but not in despair; **persecuted**, but not abandoned; **struck down**, but not destroyed. We always carry around **in our body the death of Jesus**, so that the life of Jesus may also be revealed in our body. For we who are alive are **always being given over to death for Jesus' sake**, so that his life may also be revealed in our mortal body. So then, **death is at work in us**, but life is at work in you.

Galatians 4:29: At that time the son born according to the flesh **persecuted** the son born by the power of the Spirit. It is the same now.

Galatians 5:11: Brothers and sisters, if I am still preaching circumcision, why am I still being **persecuted**? In that case the offense of the cross has been abolished.

Galatians 6:12: Those who want to impress people by means of the flesh are trying to compel you to be circumcised. The only reason they do this is **to avoid being persecuted for the cross of Christ**.

2 Corinthians 1:8-11: We do not want you to be uninformed, brothers and sisters, about the troubles we experienced in the province of Asia. We were **under great pressure, far beyond our ability to endure, so that we despaired of life itself. Indeed, we felt we had received the sentence of death.** But this happened that we might not rely on ourselves but on God, who raises the dead. He has delivered us from such a deadly peril, and he will deliver us again. On him we have set our hope that he will continue to deliver us, as you help us by your prayers. Then many will give thanks on our behalf for the gracious favor granted us in answer to the prayers of many.

THE IMPRISONED

Psalm 79:11: May the **groans of the prisoners** come before you; with your strong arm preserve those condemned to die.

Psalm 102:19-20: "The LORD looked down from his sanctuary on high, from heaven he viewed the earth, to hear the **groans of the prisoners** and release those condemned to death."

Revelation 2:10-11: Do not be afraid of what you are about to suffer. I tell you, **the devil will put some of you in prison to test you, and you will suffer persecution** for ten days. Be faithful, even to the point of death, and I will give you life as your victor's crown. Whoever has ears, let them hear what the Spirit says to the churches. The one who is victorious will not be hurt at all by the second death.

Hebrews 13:3: Continue to **remember those in prison** as if you were together with them in prison, and those who are mistreated as if you yourselves were suffering.

Hebrews 11:36-38: Some faced jeers and flogging, and even **chains and imprisonment**. They were put to death by stoning; they were sawed in two; they were killed by the sword. They went about in sheepskins and goatskins, destitute, persecuted and mistreated-- the world was not worthy of them. They wandered in deserts and mountains, living in caves and in holes in the ground.

Hebrews 10:32-36: Remember those earlier days after you had received the light, when you endured in a great conflict full of suffering. Sometimes you were publicly exposed to insult and persecution; at other times you stood side by side with those who were so treated. **You suffered along with those in prison** and joyfully accepted the confiscation of your property, because you knew that you yourselves had better and lasting possessions. So do not throw away your confidence; it will be richly rewarded. You need to persevere so that when you have done the will of God, you will receive what he has promised.

Psalm 107:10-16: Some sat in darkness, in utter darkness, **prisoners suffering in iron chains**, because they rebelled against God's commands and despised the plans of the Most High. So he subjected them to bitter labor; they stumbled, and there was no one to help. Then they cried to the LORD in their trouble, and he saved them from their distress. He brought them out of darkness, the utter darkness, and broke away their chains. Let them give thanks to the LORD for his unfailing love and his wonderful deeds for mankind, for he breaks down gates of bronze and cuts through bars of iron.

Psalm 107:10-16: Some sat in darkness, in utter darkness, **prisoners suffering in iron chains**, because they rebelled against God's commands and despised the plans of the Most High. So he subjected them to bitter labor; they stumbled, and there was no one to help. Then they cried to the LORD in their trouble, and he saved them from their distress. He brought them out of darkness, the utter darkness, and broke away their chains. Let them give thanks to the LORD for his unfailing love and his wonderful deeds for mankind, for he breaks down gates of bronze and cuts through bars of iron.

BIBLICAL MEN WHO DID TIME IN PRISON

- Joseph
- Samson
- Jeremiah
- Micaiah
- Daniel
- Daniel's friends
- John the Baptist
- Peter
- John
- Paul
- Silas
- Jesus

The Fifth Day (Thursday): The Persecuted, Poor, & Oppressed

THE POOR & NEEDY, WIDOWS & FATHERLESS/ORPHANS

Luke 6:20-21, 24-25: Looking at his disciples, he said: "**Blessed are you who are poor**, for yours is the kingdom of God. **Blessed are you who hunger now**, for you will be satisfied. **Blessed are you who weep now**, for you will laugh. ... "**But woe to you who are rich**, for you have already received your comfort. **Woe to you who are well fed now**, for you will go hungry. **Woe to you who laugh now**, for you will mourn and weep.

Luke 14:12-14: Then Jesus said to his host, "When you give a luncheon or dinner, **do not invite your friends, your brothers or sisters, your relatives, or your rich neighbors**; if you do, they may invite you back and so you will be repaid. But when you give a banquet, **invite the poor, the crippled, the lame, the blind, and you will be blessed**. Although they cannot repay you, you will be repaid at the resurrection of the righteous."

James 1:27: Religion that God our Father accepts as pure and faultless is this: **to look after orphans and widows in their distress** and to keep oneself from being polluted by the world.

Proverbs 19:17: Whoever is **kind to the poor** lends to the LORD, and he will reward them for what they have done.

James 2:1-7, 14-18: My brothers and sisters, believers in our glorious Lord Jesus Christ must not show favoritism. Suppose a man comes into your meeting wearing a gold ring and fine clothes, and a poor man in filthy old clothes also comes in. If you show special attention to the man wearing fine clothes and say, "Here's a good seat for you," but say to the poor man, "You stand there" or "Sit on the floor by my feet," have you not discriminated among yourselves and become judges with evil thoughts? Listen, my dear brothers and sisters: **Has not God chosen those who are poor in the eyes of the world to be rich in faith and to inherit the kingdom** he promised those who love him? **But you have dishonored the poor**. Is it not the rich who are exploiting you? Are they not the ones who are dragging you into court? Are they not the ones who are blaspheming the noble name of him to whom you belong? ... What good is it, my brothers and sisters, if someone claims to have faith but has no deeds? Can such faith save them? **Suppose a brother or a sister is without clothes and daily food. If one of you says to them, "Go in peace; keep warm and well fed," but does nothing about their physical needs, what good is it?** In the same way, faith by itself, if it is not accompanied by action, is dead. But someone will say, "You have faith; I have deeds." Show me your faith without deeds, and I will show you my faith by my deeds.

Isaiah 58:6-12: "Is not this the kind of fasting I have chosen: to **loose the chains of injustice** and **untie the cords of the yoke**, to **set the oppressed free and break every yoke**? Is it not to **share your food with the hungry and to provide the poor wanderer with shelter--when you see the naked, to clothe them, and not to turn away from your own flesh and blood**? Then your light will break forth like the dawn, and your healing will quickly appear; then your righteousness will go before you, and the glory of the LORD will be your rear guard. Then you will call, and the LORD will answer; you will cry for help, and he will say: Here am I. "If you do away with the yoke of oppression, with the pointing finger and malicious talk, and **if you spend yourselves in behalf of the hungry and satisfy the needs of the oppressed**, then your light will rise in the darkness, and your night will become like the noonday. The LORD will guide you always; he will satisfy your needs in a sun-scorched land and will strengthen your frame. You will be like a well-watered garden, like a spring whose waters never fail. Your people will rebuild the ancient ruins and will raise up the age-old foundations; you will be called Repairer of Broken Walls, Restorer of Streets with Dwellings.

Exodus 22:22-24: "**Do not take advantage of the widow or the fatherless**. If you do and they cry out to me, I will certainly hear their cry. My anger will be aroused, and I will kill you with the sword; your wives will become widows and your children fatherless.

Exodus 22:25-27: "**If you lend money to one of my people among you who is needy**, do not treat it like a business deal; charge no interest. If you take your neighbor's cloak as a pledge, return it by sunset, because that cloak is the only covering your neighbor has. What else can they sleep in? When they cry out to me, I will hear, for I am compassionate.

Deuteronomy 15:7-8, 10-11: **If anyone is poor among your fellow Israelites** in any of the towns of the land the LORD your God is giving you, do not be hardhearted or tightfisted toward them. Rather, be openhanded and freely lend them whatever they need. ... Give generously to them and do so without a grudging heart; then because of this the LORD your God will bless you in all your work and in everything you put your hand to. There will always be poor people in the land. Therefore I command you to **be openhanded toward your fellow Israelites who are poor and needy in your land**.

Deuteronomy 24:10-15: When you make a loan of any kind to your neighbor, do not go into their house to get what is offered to you as a pledge. Stay outside and let the neighbor to whom you are making the loan bring the pledge out to you. **If the neighbor is poor**, do not go to sleep with their pledge in your possession. Return their cloak by sunset so that your neighbor may sleep in it. Then they will thank you, and it will be regarded as a righteous act in the sight of the LORD your God. **Do not take advantage of a hired worker who is poor and needy, whether that worker is a fellow Israelite or a foreigner residing in one of your towns**. Pay them their wages each day before sunset, because they are poor and are counting on it. Otherwise they may cry to the LORD against you, and you will be guilty of sin.

Psalm 9:18: But **God will never forget the needy**; the hope of the afflicted will never perish.

Psalm 10:13-18: Why does the wicked man revile God? Why does he say to himself, "He won't call me to account"? **But you, God, see the trouble of the afflicted; you consider their grief** and take it in hand. The victims commit themselves to you; **you are the helper of the fatherless**. Break the arm of the wicked man; call the evildoer to account for his wickedness that would not otherwise be found out. The LORD is King for ever and ever; the nations will perish from his land. **You, LORD, hear the desire of the afflicted**; you encourage them, and you listen to their cry, **defending the fatherless and the oppressed**, so that mere earthly mortals will never again strike terror.

The Fifth Day (Thursday): The Persecuted, Poor, & Oppressed

Psalm 12:5: "**Because the poor are plundered and the needy groan**, I will now arise," says the LORD. "I will protect them from those who malign them."

Psalm 14:6: You evildoers frustrate the **plans of the poor**, but the LORD is their refuge.

Psalm 35:10: My whole being will exclaim, "Who is like you, LORD? **You rescue the poor** from those too strong for them, **the poor and needy** from those who rob them."

Psalm 37:14: The wicked draw the sword and bend the bow to bring down **the poor and needy**, to slay those whose ways are upright.

Psalm 40:17: But as for me, **I am poor and needy**; may the Lord think of me. You are my help and my deliverer; you are my God, do not delay.

Psalm 82:1-4: God presides in the great assembly; he renders judgment among the "gods": "How long will you defend the unjust and show partiality to the wicked? **Defend the weak and the fatherless; uphold the cause of the poor and the oppressed. Rescue the weak and the needy**; deliver them from the hand of the wicked.

Proverbs 22:22-23: **Do not exploit the poor because they are poor** and do not crush the needy in court, for the LORD will take up their case and will exact life for life.

Proverbs 31:9: Speak up and judge fairly; defend **the rights of the poor and needy**.

Isaiah 1:17: Learn to do right; seek justice. Defend the oppressed. **Take up the cause of the fatherless; plead the case of the widow**.

Isaiah 41:17-20: "**The poor and needy** search for water, but there is none; their tongues are parched with thirst. But I the LORD will answer them; I, the God of Israel, will not forsake them. I will make rivers flow on barren heights, and springs within the valleys. I will turn the desert into pools of water, and the parched ground into springs. I will put in the desert the cedar and the acacia, the myrtle and the olive. I will set junipers in the wasteland, the fir and the cypress together, so that people may see and know, may consider and understand, that the hand of the LORD has done this, that the Holy One of Israel has created it.

Jeremiah 7:5-7: If you really change your ways and your actions and deal with each other justly, **if you do not oppress the foreigner, the fatherless or the widow** and do not shed innocent blood in this place, and if you do not follow other gods to your own harm, then I will let you live in this place, in the land I gave your ancestors for ever and ever.

Jeremiah 22:3, 13-17: This is what the LORD says: Do what is just and right. Rescue from the hand of the oppressor the one who has been robbed. **Do no wrong or violence to the foreigner, the fatherless or the widow**, and do not shed innocent blood in this place. ...13-17 "Woe to him who builds his palace by unrighteousness, his upper rooms by injustice, making his own people work for nothing, not paying them for their labor. He says, 'I will build myself a great palace with spacious upper rooms.' So he makes large windows in it, panels it with cedar and decorates it in red. "Does it make you a king to have more and more cedar? Did not your father [Josiah] have food and drink? He did what was right and just, so all went well with him. **He defended the cause of the poor and needy, and so all went well. Is that not what it means to know me?**" declares the LORD. "But your eyes and your heart are set only on dishonest gain, on shedding innocent blood and on oppression and extortion."

Ezekiel 16:49-50: " 'Now this was the sin of your sister Sodom: She and her daughters were arrogant, overfed and unconcerned; **they did not help the poor and needy**. They were haughty and did detestable things before me. Therefore I did away with them as you have seen.

Zechariah 7:9-10: "This is what the LORD Almighty said: 'Administer true justice; show mercy and compassion to one another. **Do not oppress the widow or the fatherless, the foreigner or the poor**. Do not plot evil against each other.'

Mark 12:38-40: As he taught, Jesus said, "Watch out for the teachers of the law. They like to walk around in flowing robes and be greeted with respect in the marketplaces, and have the most important seats in the synagogues and the places of honor at banquets. **They devour widows' houses** and for a show make lengthy prayers. These men will be punished most severely."

Job's Self Defense:
Job 31:16-28: "If I have denied the desires of **the poor** or let the eyes of **the widow** grow weary, if I have **kept my bread to myself, not sharing it with the fatherless**-- but from my youth I reared them as a father would, and from my birth I guided the widow-- if I have seen **anyone perishing for lack of clothing, or the needy without garments**, and their hearts did not bless me for warming them with the fleece from my sheep, if I have raised my hand against **the fatherless**, knowing that I had influence in court, then let my arm fall from the shoulder, let it be broken off at the joint. **For I dreaded destruction from God, and for fear of his splendor I could not do such things.** If I have put my trust in gold or said to pure gold, 'You are my security,' if I have rejoiced over my great wealth, the fortune my hands had gained, if I have regarded the sun in its radiance or the moon moving in splendor, so that my heart was secretly enticed and my hand offered them a kiss of homage, then these also would be sins to be judged, for I would have been unfaithful to God on high.

Parable of the Rich Fool:
Luke 12:13-21: Someone in the crowd said to him, "Teacher, tell my brother to divide the inheritance with me." Jesus replied, "Man, who appointed me a judge or an arbiter between you?" Then he said to them, "Watch out! Be on your guard against all kinds of greed; life does not consist in an abundance of possessions." And he told them this parable: "The ground of a certain rich man yielded an abundant harvest. He thought to himself, 'What shall I do? I have no place to store my crops.' "Then he said, 'This is what I'll do. I will tear down my barns and build bigger ones, and there I will store my surplus grain. And I'll say to myself, "You have plenty of grain laid up for many years. Take life easy; eat,

drink and be merry." ' "But God said to him, 'You fool! This very night your life will be demanded from you. Then who will get what you have prepared for yourself?' **This is how it will be with whoever stores up things for themselves but is not rich toward God**."

Parable of the Rich Man and Lazarus:
Luke 16:19-31: "There was a rich man who was **dressed in purple and fine linen and lived in luxury** every day. At his gate was laid **a beggar named Lazarus**, covered with sores and longing to eat what fell from the rich man's table. Even the dogs came and licked his sores. "The time came when **the beggar** died and the angels carried him to Abraham's side. The **rich man also died** and was buried. In Hades, where he was in torment, he looked up and saw Abraham far away, with Lazarus by his side. So he called to him, 'Father Abraham, have pity on me and send Lazarus to dip the tip of his finger in water and cool my tongue, because I am in agony in this fire.' "But Abraham replied, 'Son, remember that in your lifetime you received your good things, while Lazarus received bad things, but now he is comforted here and you are in agony. And besides all this, between us and you a great chasm has been set in place, so that those who want to go from here to you cannot, nor can anyone cross over from there to us.' "He answered, 'Then I beg you, father, send Lazarus to my family, for I have five brothers. Let him warn them, so that they will not also come to this place of torment.' "Abraham replied, 'They have Moses and the Prophets; let them listen to them.' " 'No, father Abraham,' he said, 'but if someone from the dead goes to them, they will repent.' "He said to him, 'If they do not listen to Moses and the Prophets, they will not be convinced even if someone rises from the dead.' "

Parable of the Sheep and the Goats:
Matthew 25:31-46: "When the Son of Man comes in his glory, and all the angels with him, he will sit on his glorious throne. All the nations will be gathered before him, and he will separate the people one from another as a shepherd separates the sheep from the goats. He will put the sheep on his right and the goats on his left. "Then the King will say to those on his right, 'Come, you who are blessed by my Father; take your inheritance, the kingdom prepared for you since the creation of the world. **For I was hungry and you gave me something to eat, I was thirsty and you gave me something to drink, I was a stranger and you invited me in, I needed clothes and you clothed me, I was sick and you looked after me, I was in prison and you came to visit me**.' "Then the righteous will answer him, 'Lord, when did we see you hungry and feed you, or thirsty and give you something to drink? When did we see you a stranger and invite you in, or needing clothes and clothe you? When did we see you sick or in prison and go to visit you?' "The King will reply, **'Truly I tell you, whatever you did for one of the least of these brothers and sisters of mine, you did for me**.' "Then he will say to those on his left, 'Depart from me, you who are cursed, into the eternal fire prepared for the devil and his angels. **For I was hungry and you gave me nothing to eat, I was thirsty and you gave me nothing to drink, I was a stranger and you did not invite me in, I needed clothes and you did not clothe me, I was sick and in prison and you did not look after me**.' "They also will answer, 'Lord, when did we see you hungry or thirsty or a stranger or needing clothes or sick or in prison, and did not help you?' "He will reply, **'Truly I tell you, whatever you did not do for one of the least of these, you did not do for me**.' "Then they will go away to eternal punishment, but the righteous to eternal life."

Daily Prayer Focus

---

1 Corinthians 7:8-9: Now to the unmarried and the **widows** I say: It is good for them to stay unmarried, as I do. But if they cannot control themselves, they should marry, for it is better to marry than to burn with passion.

1 Timothy 5:3-16: Give proper recognition to those **widows** who are really in need. But if a **widow** has children or grandchildren, these should learn first of all to put their religion into practice by caring for their own family and so repaying their parents and grandparents, for this is pleasing to God. The widow who is really in need and left all alone puts her hope in God and continues night and day to pray and to ask God for help. But the widow who lives for pleasure is dead even while she lives. Give the people these instructions, so that no one may be open to blame. Anyone who does not provide for their relatives, and especially for their own household, has denied the faith and is worse than an unbeliever. **No widow** may be put on the list of widows unless she is over sixty, has been faithful to her husband, and is well known for her good deeds, such as bringing up children, showing hospitality, washing the feet of the Lord's people, helping those in trouble and devoting herself to all kinds of good deeds. As for **younger widows**, do not put them on such a list. For when their sensual desires overcome their dedication to Christ, they want to marry. Thus they bring judgment on themselves, because they have broken their first pledge. Besides, they get into the habit of being idle and going about from house to house. And not only do they become idlers, but also busybodies who talk nonsense, saying things they ought not to. So I counsel **younger widows** to marry, to have children, to manage their homes and to give the enemy no opportunity for slander. Some have in fact already turned away to follow Satan. If any woman who is a believer has **widows in her care**, she should continue to help them and not let the church be burdened with them, so that the church can help those **widows who are really in need**.

Leviticus 19:10: Do not go over your vineyard a second time or pick up the grapes that have fallen. **Leave them for the poor and the foreigner**. I am the LORD your God.

Deuteronomy 24:17-22: **Do not deprive the foreigner or the fatherless of justice, or take the cloak of the widow as a pledge.** Remember that you were slaves in Egypt and the LORD your God redeemed you from there. That is why I command you to do this. When you are harvesting in your field and you overlook a sheaf, do not go back to get it. **Leave it for the foreigner, the fatherless and the widow**, so that the LORD your God may bless you in all the work of your hands. When you beat the olives from your trees, do not go over the branches a second time. **Leave what remains for the foreigner, the fatherless and the widow**. When you harvest the grapes in your vineyard, do not go over the vines again. **Leave what remains for the foreigner, the fatherless and the widow**. Remember that you were slaves in Egypt. That is why I command you to do this.

THE SICK (OPPRESSED BY THE DEVIL)

Isaiah 53:3-5: He was despised and rejected by mankind, a man of suffering, and familiar with pain. Like one from whom people hide their faces he was despised, and we held him in low esteem. Surely he took up our pain and bore our suffering, yet we considered him

The Fifth Day (Thursday): The Persecuted, Poor, & Oppressed

punished by God, stricken by him, and afflicted. But he was pierced for our transgressions, he was crushed for our iniquities; the punishment that brought us peace was on him, and **by his wounds we are healed.**

1 Peter 2:24: He himself bore our sins" in his body on the cross, so that we might die to sins and live for righteousness; "**by his wounds you have been healed.**"

Psalm 6:2: Have mercy on me, LORD, for I am faint; heal me, LORD, for **my bones are in agony.**

Psalm 41:1-3: **Blessed are those who have regard for the weak [poor]**; the LORD delivers them in times of trouble. The LORD protects and preserves them--they are counted among the blessed in the land--he does not give them over to the desire of their foes. **The LORD sustains them on their sickbed and restores them from their bed of illness.**

Psalm 35:13-14: **Yet when they were ill**, I put on sackcloth and humbled myself with fasting. When my prayers returned to me unanswered, I went about mourning as though for my friend or brother. I bowed my head in grief as though weeping for my mother.

Ezekiel 34:2-4, 15-16: "Son of man, prophesy against the shepherds of Israel; prophesy and say to them: 'This is what the Sovereign LORD says: Woe to you shepherds of Israel who only take care of yourselves! Should not shepherds take care of the flock? You eat the curds, clothe yourselves with the wool and slaughter the choice animals, but you do not take care of the flock. **You have not strengthened the weak or healed the sick or bound up the injured.** You have not brought back the strays or searched for the lost. You have ruled them harshly and brutally. ... I myself will tend my sheep and have them lie down, declares the Sovereign LORD. I will search for the lost and bring back the strays. **I will bind up the injured and strengthen the weak, but the sleek and the strong I will destroy.** I will shepherd the flock with justice.

Psalm 30:2: LORD my God, I called to you for help, and **you healed me.**

Psalm 41:4: I said, "Have mercy on me, LORD; **heal me**, for I have sinned against you."

Psalm 103:1-5: Praise the LORD, my soul; all my inmost being, praise his holy name. Praise the LORD, my soul, and forget not all his benefits-- who forgives all your sins and **heals all your diseases**, who redeems your life from the pit and crowns you with love and compassion, who satisfies your desires with good things so that your youth is renewed like the eagle's.

Psalm 107:20: He sent out his word and **healed them**; he rescued them from the grave.

Psalm 147:3: He **heals** the brokenhearted and **binds up their wounds.**

Matthew 8:16: When evening came, many who were demon-possessed were brought to him, and he drove out the spirits with a word and **healed all the sick.**

Matthew 9:12: On hearing this, Jesus said, "**It is not the healthy who need a doctor, but the sick.**

Matthew 14:14, 35: When Jesus landed and saw a large crowd, he had compassion on them and **healed their sick**. ... And when the men of that place recognized Jesus, they sent word to all the surrounding country. **People brought all their sick to him**

Mark 1:32-34: That evening after sunset the people brought to Jesus **all the sick and demon-possessed**. The whole town gathered at the door, and **Jesus healed many who had various diseases**. He also drove out many demons, but he would not let the demons speak because they knew who he was.

Mark 6:13: They **drove out many demons** and **anointed many sick people with oil and healed them**.

Mark 16:17-18: And these signs will accompany those who believe: In my name they will **drive out demons**; they will speak in new tongues; they will pick up snakes with their hands; and when they drink deadly poison, it will not hurt them at all; **they will place their hands on sick people, and they will get well.**"

Matthew 4:24: News about him spread all over Syria, and people brought to him all who were ill with **various diseases, those suffering severe pain, the demon-possessed, those having seizures, and the paralyzed; and he healed them**.

Matthew 9:35: Jesus went through all the towns and villages, teaching in their synagogues, proclaiming the good news of the kingdom and **healing every disease and sickness**.

Matthew 10:1: Jesus called his twelve disciples to him and gave them **authority to drive out impure spirits and to heal every disease and sickness**.

Luke 9:1: When Jesus had called the Twelve together, he **gave them power and authority to drive out all demons and to cure diseases**,

Acts 5:15-16: As a result, people brought the sick into the streets and laid them on beds and mats so that at least Peter's shadow might fall on some of them as he passed by. Crowds gathered also from the towns around Jerusalem, **bringing their sick and those tormented by impure spirits, and all of them were healed**.

Acts 10:38: how God anointed Jesus of Nazareth with the Holy Spirit and power, and how he went around **doing good and healing all who were under the power of the devil**, because God was with him.

Acts 19:11-12: God did extraordinary miracles through Paul, so that even handkerchiefs and aprons that had touched him were **taken to the sick, and their illnesses were cured and the evil spirits left them**.

The Fifth Day (Thursday): The Persecuted, Poor, & Oppressed

1 Corinthians 11:28-30: Everyone ought to examine themselves before they eat of the bread and drink from the cup. For those who eat and drink without discerning the body of Christ eat and drink judgment on themselves. **That is why many among you are weak and sick, and a number of you have fallen asleep [died].**

The Sixth Day (Friday)
FAMILY & FRIENDS, NEIGHBORS & ENEMIES

INDEX OF TOPICS:
- Household Salvation (Natural Family)
- Marriage
- Mothers & Fathers, Children, Brothers & Sisters (Natural Family)
- The Family of Believers
- One Another & Unity Scriptures
- Loving God More than Family
- Friends
- Neighbors
- Enemies

HOUSEHOLD SALVATION (NATURAL FAMILY)

Genesis 7:1: The LORD then said to Noah, "Go into the ark, **you and your whole family**, because I have found you righteous in this generation."

Hebrews 11:7: By faith Noah, when warned about things not yet seen, in holy fear built an ark to **save his family**. By his faith he condemned the world and became heir of the righteousness that is in keeping with faith.

Joshua 6:25 ESV: But **Rahab the prostitute and her father's household and all who belonged to her**, Joshua saved alive. And she has lived in Israel to this day, because she hid the messengers whom Joshua sent to spy out Jericho.

Joshua 24:14-15: "Now fear the LORD and serve him with all faithfulness. Throw away the gods your ancestors worshiped beyond the Euphrates River and in Egypt, and serve the LORD. But if serving the LORD seems undesirable to you, then choose for yourselves this day whom you will serve, whether the gods your ancestors served beyond the Euphrates, or the gods of the Amorites, in whose land you are living. **But as for me and my household**, we will serve the LORD."

Acts 16:27-34: The jailer woke up, and when he saw the prison doors open, he drew his sword and was about to kill himself because he thought the prisoners had escaped. But Paul shouted, "Don't harm yourself! We are all here!" The jailer called for lights, rushed in and fell trembling before Paul and Silas. He then brought them out and asked, "Sirs, what must I do to be saved?" They replied, "Believe in the Lord Jesus, and you will be saved – you and your household." Then they spoke the word of the Lord to him and to all the others in his house. At that hour of the night the jailer took them and washed their wounds; then immediately he and all his household were baptized. The jailer brought them into his house and set a meal before them; he was filled with joy because he had come to believe in God – **he and his whole household**.

John 4:50-53: "Go," Jesus replied, "your son will live." The man took Jesus at his word and departed. While he was still on the way, his servants met him with the news that his boy was living. When he inquired as to the time when his son got better, they said to him, "Yesterday, at one in the afternoon, the fever left him." Then the father realized that this was the exact time at which Jesus had said to him, "Your son will live." **So he and his whole household believed**.

Acts 10:24, 44: The following day he arrived in Caesarea. Cornelius was expecting them and had **called together his relatives and close friends**. ... While Peter was still speaking these words, the Holy Spirit came on all who heard the message.

Acts 11:14: He will bring you a message through which **you and all your household will be saved**.

Acts 18:8: **Crispus, the synagogue leader, and his entire household** believed in the Lord; and many of the Corinthians who heard Paul believed and were baptized.

1 Corinthians 1:16: (Yes, I also baptized the **household of Stephanas**; beyond that, I don't remember if I baptized anyone else.)
1 Corinthians 16:15: You know that the **household of Stephanas** were the first converts in Achaia, and they have devoted themselves to the service of the Lord's people. I urge you, brothers and sisters, to submit to such people and to everyone who joins in the work and labors at it.

MARRIAGE

Hebrews 13:4: **Marriage should be honored by all**, and the marriage bed kept pure, for God will judge the adulterer and all the sexually immoral.

Colossians 3:18-19: **Wives, submit yourselves to your husbands**, as is fitting in the Lord. **Husbands, love your wives** and do not be harsh with them.

1 Peter 3:1-7: **Wives, in the same way submit yourselves to your own husbands** so that, if any of them do not believe the word, they may be won over without words by the behavior of their wives, when they see the purity and reverence of your lives. Your beauty should not come from outward adornment, such as elaborate hairstyles and the wearing of gold jewelry or fine clothes. Rather, it should be that of your inner self, the unfading beauty of a gentle and quiet spirit, which is of great worth in God's sight. **For this is the way**

Daily Prayer Focus

the holy women of the past who put their hope in God used to adorn themselves. They submitted themselves to their own husbands, like Sarah, who obeyed Abraham and called him her lord. You are her daughters if you do what is right and do not give way to fear. **Husbands, in the same way be considerate as you live with your wives,** and treat them with respect as the weaker partner and as heirs with you of the gracious gift of life, so that nothing will hinder your prayers.

Ephesians 5:22-32: **Wives, submit to your own husbands,** as to the Lord. For the **husband is the head of the wife** even as Christ is the head of the church, his body, and is himself its Savior. Now as the church submits to Christ, so also wives should submit in everything to their husbands. **Husbands, love your wives, as Christ loved the church and gave himself up for her,** that he might sanctify her, having cleansed her by the washing of water with the word, so that he might present the church to himself in splendor, without spot or wrinkle or any such thing, that she might be holy and without blemish. In the same way **husbands should love their wives as their own bodies.** He who loves his wife loves himself. For no one ever hated his own flesh, but nourishes and cherishes it, just as Christ does the church, because we are members of his body. "**Therefore a man shall leave his father and mother and hold fast to his wife, and the two shall become one flesh.**" This mystery is profound, and I am saying that it refers to Christ and the church.

Genesis 2:22-25: And the rib that the LORD God had taken from the man he made into a woman and brought her to the man. Then the man said, "**This at last is bone of my bones and flesh of my flesh**; she shall be called Woman, because she was taken out of Man." **Therefore a man shall leave his father and his mother and hold fast to his wife, and they shall become one flesh.** And the man and his wife were both naked and were not ashamed.

Matthew 19:3-12: Some Pharisees came to him to test him. They asked, "Is it lawful for a man to divorce his wife for any and every reason?" "Haven't you read," he replied, "that at the beginning the Creator 'made them male and female,' and said, 'For this reason a man will leave his father and mother and be united to his wife, and the two will become one flesh'? So they are no longer two, but one flesh. **Therefore what God has joined together, let no one separate.**" "Why then," they asked, "did Moses command that a man give his wife a certificate of divorce and send her away?" Jesus replied, "**Moses permitted you to divorce your wives because your hearts were hard. But it was not this way from the beginning. I tell you that anyone who divorces his wife, except for sexual immorality, and marries another woman commits adultery.**" The disciples said to him, "If this is the situation between a husband and wife, it is better not to marry." Jesus replied, "Not everyone can accept this word, but only those to whom it has been given. For there are eunuchs who were born that way, and there are eunuchs who have been made eunuchs by others-- and there are those who choose to live like eunuchs for the sake of the kingdom of heaven. The one who can accept this should accept it."

Mark 10:2-12: Some Pharisees came and tested him by asking, "Is it lawful for a man to divorce his wife?" "What did Moses command you?" he replied. They said, "Moses permitted a man to write a certificate of divorce and send her away." "It was because your hearts were hard that Moses wrote you this law," Jesus replied. "**But at the beginning**

The Sixth Day (Friday): Family & Friends, Neighbors & Enemies

of creation God 'made them male and female.' 'For this reason a man will leave his father and mother and be united to his wife, and the two will become one flesh.' So they are no longer two, but one flesh. Therefore what God has joined together, let no one separate." When they were in the house again, the disciples asked Jesus about this. He answered, "**Anyone who divorces his wife and marries another woman commits adultery against her. And if she divorces her husband and marries another man, she commits adultery.**"

Matthew 5:31-32: It has been said, 'Anyone who divorces his wife must give her a certificate of divorce.' **But I tell you that anyone who divorces his wife, except for sexual immorality, makes her the victim of adultery, and anyone who marries a divorced woman commits adultery.**

Matthew 5:27-30: You have heard that it was said, **'You shall not commit adultery.'** But I tell you that **anyone who looks at a woman lustfully has already committed adultery with her in his heart.** If your right eye causes you to stumble, gouge it out and throw it away. It is better for you to lose one part of your body than for your whole body to be thrown into hell. And if your right hand causes you to stumble, cut it off and throw it away. It is better for you to lose one part of your body than for your whole body to go into hell.

1 Corinthians 7:1-9: Now for the matters you wrote about: "It is good for a man not to have sexual relations with a woman." But since sexual immorality is occurring, **each man should have sexual relations with his own wife, and each woman with her own husband.** The husband should fulfill his marital duty to his wife, and likewise the wife to her husband. **The wife does not have authority over her own body** but yields it to her husband. In the same way, **the husband does not have authority over his own body** but yields it to his wife. **Do not deprive each other except perhaps by mutual consent and for a time, so that you may devote yourselves to prayer.** Then come together again so that Satan will not tempt you because of your lack of self-control. I say this as a concession, not as a command. I wish that all of you were as I am. But each of you has your own gift from God; one has this gift, another has that.

1 Corinthians 7:8-9: Now **to the unmarried and the widows I say: It is good for them to stay unmarried**, as I do. But if they cannot control themselves, they should marry, for **it is better to marry than to burn with passion.**

1 Corinthians 7:10-16: **To the married** I give this command (not I, but the Lord): **A wife must not separate from her husband.** But if she does, she must remain unmarried or else be reconciled to her husband. **And a husband must not divorce his wife.** To the rest I say this (I, not the Lord): If any brother has a wife who is not a believer and she is willing to live with him, **he must not divorce her.** And if a woman has a husband who is not a believer and he is willing to live with her, **she must not divorce him.** For the unbelieving husband has been sanctified through his wife, and the unbelieving wife has been sanctified through her believing husband. Otherwise your children would be unclean, but as it is, they are holy. But if the unbeliever leaves, let it be so. The brother or the sister is not bound in such circumstances; God has called us to live in peace. **How do you know, wife, whether you will save your husband? Or, how do you know, husband, whether you will save your wife?**

1 Corinthians 7:27-31: Are you pledged to a woman? Do not seek to be released. Are you free from such a commitment? **Do not look for a wife. But if you do marry**, you have not sinned; and if a virgin marries, she has not sinned. **But those who marry will face many troubles in this life, and I want to spare you this**. What I mean, brothers and sisters, is that the time is short. From now on **those who have wives should live as if they do not**; those who mourn, as if they did not; those who are happy, as if they were not; those who buy something, as if it were not theirs to keep; those who use the things of the world, as if not engrossed in them. For this world in its present form is passing away.

1 Corinthians 7:32-40: I would like you to be free from concern. **An unmarried man** is concerned about the Lord's affairs--how he can please the Lord. **But a married man** is concerned about the affairs of this world--how he can please his wife-- and his interests are divided. **An unmarried woman or virgin** is concerned about the Lord's affairs: Her aim is to be devoted to the Lord in both body and spirit. **But a married woman** is concerned about the affairs of this world--how she can please her husband. **I am saying this for your own good, not to restrict you, but that you may live in a right way in undivided devotion to the Lord**. If anyone is worried that he might not be acting honorably toward the virgin he is engaged to, and if his passions are too strong and he feels he ought to marry, he should do as he wants. He is not sinning. They should get married. But the man who has settled the matter in his own mind, who is under no compulsion but has control over his own will, and who has made up his mind not to marry the virgin--this man also does the right thing. **So then, he who marries the virgin does right, but he who does not marry her does better. A woman is bound to her husband as long as he lives. But if her husband dies, she is free to marry anyone she wishes, but he must belong to the Lord**. In my judgment, she is happier if she stays as she is--and I think that I too have the Spirit of God.

Titus 2:1-6: You, however, must teach what is appropriate to sound doctrine. Teach the older men to be temperate, worthy of respect, self-controlled, and sound in faith, in love and in endurance. Likewise, teach the older women to be reverent in the way they live, not to be slanderers or addicted to much wine, but to teach what is good. Then they can **urge the younger women to love their husbands and children, to be self-controlled and pure, to be busy at home, to be kind, and to be subject to their husbands**, so that no one will malign the word of God. Similarly, encourage the young men to be self-controlled.

MOTHERS & FATHERS, CHILDREN, BROTHERS & SISTERS (NATURAL FAMILY)

Exodus 20:12: **Honor your father and your mother**, so that you may live long in the land the LORD your God is giving you.

Exodus 21:17: Anyone who **curses their father or mother** is to be put to death.

Leviticus 20:9: Anyone who **curses their father or mother** is to be put to death. Because they have cursed their father or mother, their blood will be on their own head.

Ephesians 6:1-4: **Children, obey your parents in the Lord,** for this is right. "**Honor your father** and mother"--which is the first commandment with a promise-- "so that it may go well with you and that you may enjoy long life on the earth." **Fathers, do not exasperate your children**; instead, bring them up in the training and instruction of the Lord.

Colossians 3:20-21: **Children, obey your parents in everything**, for this pleases the Lord. **Fathers, do not embitter your children**, or they will become discouraged.

Genesis 4:9: Then the LORD said to Cain, "Where is your brother Abel?" "I don't know," he replied. "**Am I my brother's keeper?**"

Deuteronomy 23:7: Do not despise an Edomite, for the Edomites are **related to you**. Do not despise an Egyptian, because you resided as foreigners in their country.

Matthew 5:22: But I tell you that anyone who is **angry with a brother or sister** will be subject to judgment. Again, anyone who **says to a brother or sister, 'Raca,'** is answerable to the court. And anyone who says, 'You fool!' will be in danger of the fire of hell.

FAMILY OF BELIEVERS

Mark 3:21, 31-35: When his [Jesus] family heard about this, they went to take charge of him, for they said, "He is out of his mind." ... Then Jesus' mother and brothers arrived. Standing outside, they sent someone in to call him. A crowd was sitting around him, and they told him, "Your mother and brothers are outside looking for you." "**Who are my mother and my brothers?**" he asked. Then he looked at those seated in a circle around him and said, "Here are my mother and my brothers! **Whoever does God's will is my brother and sister and mother.**" (See also Matthew 12:48; Luke 7:5, 8:21.)

Ephesians 2:19-20: Consequently, you are no longer foreigners and strangers, but fellow citizens with God's people and also **members of his household**, built on the foundation of the apostles and prophets, with Christ Jesus himself as the chief cornerstone.

Galatians 6:10: Therefore, as we have opportunity, let us do good to all people, **especially to those who belong to the family of believers**.

1 Timothy 5:1-2: Do not rebuke an older man harshly, but exhort him as if he were your **father**. Treat younger men as **brothers**, older women as **mothers**, and younger women as **sisters**, with absolute purity.

Matthew 7:2-5: For in the same way you judge others, you will be judged, and with the measure you use, it will be measured to you. "Why do you look at the **speck of sawdust in your brother's eye** and pay no attention to the plank in your own eye? **How can you say to your brother, 'Let me take the speck out of your eye,**' when all the time there is a plank in your own eye? You hypocrite, first take the plank out of your own eye, and then you will see clearly to remove the speck from **your brother's eye**.

Matthew 18:15-17: "**If your brother or sister sins**, go and point out their fault, just between the two of you. If they listen to you, you have won them over. But if they will not listen, take one or two others along, so that 'every matter may be established by the testimony of two or three witnesses.' If they still refuse to listen, tell it to the church; and if they refuse to listen even to the church, treat them as you would a pagan or a tax collector.

Romans 14:10, 13, 15: You, then, why do you judge your **brother or sister**? Or why do you treat them with contempt? For we will all stand before God's judgment seat. ... Therefore let us stop passing judgment on one another. Instead, make up your mind not to put any stumbling block or obstacle in the way of a **brother or sister**. ... If your **brother or sister** is distressed because of what you eat, you are no longer acting in love. Do not by your eating destroy someone for whom Christ died.

Galatians 6:1-2: **Brothers and sisters**, if someone is caught in a sin, you who live by the Spirit should restore that person gently. But watch yourselves, or you also may be tempted. Carry each other's burdens, and in this way you will fulfill the law of Christ.

1 Corinthians 6:1-8: **If any of you has a dispute with another**, do you dare to take it before the ungodly for judgment instead of before the Lord's people? Or do you not know that the Lord's people will judge the world? And if you are to judge the world, are you not competent to judge trivial cases? Do you not know that we will judge angels? How much more the things of this life! Therefore, if you have disputes about such matters, do you ask for a ruling from those whose way of life is scorned in the church? I say this to shame you. Is it possible that there is nobody among you wise enough to judge a dispute between believers? But instead, one brother takes another to court--and this in front of unbelievers! **The very fact that you have lawsuits among you means you have been completely defeated already. Why not rather be wronged? Why not rather be cheated?** Instead, you yourselves cheat and do wrong, and you do this to your **brothers and sisters**.

1 John 2:10-11: Anyone who **loves their brother and sister** lives in the light, and there is nothing in them to make them stumble. But anyone who **hates a brother or sister** is in the darkness and walks around in the darkness. They do not know where they are going, because the darkness has blinded them.

1 John 3:10-16: This is how we know who the children of God are and who the children of the devil are: Anyone who does not do what is right is not God's child, **nor is anyone who does not love their brother and sister**. For this is the message you heard from the beginning: We should love one another. **Do not be like Cain, who belonged to the evil one and murdered his brother**. And why did he murder him? Because his own actions were evil and his brother's were righteous. Do not be surprised, **my brothers and sisters**, if the world hates you. We know that we have passed from death to life, because we love each other. Anyone who does not love remains in death. Anyone who **hates a brother or sister is a murderer**, and you know that no murderer has eternal life residing in him. This is how we know what love is: Jesus Christ laid down his life for us. And **we ought to lay down our lives for our brothers and sisters**.

1 John 4:19-21: We love because he first loved us. Whoever claims to love God yet **hates a brother or sister** is a liar. For whoever **does not love their brother and sister**, whom they have seen, cannot love God, whom they have not seen. And he has given us this command: **Anyone who loves God must also love their brother and sister.**

ONE ANOTHER & UNITY SCRIPTURES

John 13:14: Now that I, your Lord and Teacher, have washed your feet, you also should **wash one another's feet**.

John 15:12, 17: My command is this: **Love each other as I have loved you**. ... This is my command: **Love each other**.

Mark 9:50: "Salt is good, but if it loses its saltiness, how can you make it salty again? Have salt among yourselves, and **be at peace with each other**."

Romans 12:10, 16: **Be devoted to one another in love. Honor one another** above yourselves. ... **Live in harmony with one another**. Do not be proud, but be willing to associate with people of low position. Do not be conceited.

Galatians 5:13-15: You, my brothers and sisters, were called to be free. But do not use your freedom to indulge the flesh; rather, **serve one another humbly in love**. For the entire law is fulfilled in keeping this one command: "**Love your neighbor as yourself**." If you bite and devour each other, watch out or you will be destroyed by each other.

Ephesians 4:2, 32: Be completely humble and gentle; be patient, **bearing with one another in love**. ... **Be kind and compassionate to one another, forgiving each other**, just as in Christ God forgave you.

Ephesians 5:21: **Submit to one another** out of reverence for Christ.

Colossians 3:9, 13: **Do not lie to each other**, since you have taken off your old self with its practices ... **Bear with each other and forgive one another** if any of you has a grievance against someone. Forgive as the Lord forgave you.

1 Thessalonians 3:12: May the Lord make your **love increase and overflow for each other** and for everyone else, just as ours does for you.

1 Thessalonians 5:11: Therefore **encourage one another and build each other up**, just as in fact you are doing.

Hebrews 10:24-25: And let us consider how we may **spur one another on toward love and good deeds**, not giving up meeting together, as some are in the habit of doing, but **encouraging one another** – and all the more as you see the Day approaching.

James 4:11: Brothers and sisters, **do not slander one another**. Anyone who **speaks against a brother or sister or judges them** speaks against the law and judges it. When you judge the law, you are not keeping it, but sitting in judgment on it.

James 5:9: **Don't grumble against one another, brothers and sisters**, or you will be judged. The Judge is standing at the door!

James 5:16: Therefore **confess your sins to each other and pray for each other** so that you may be healed. The prayer of a righteous person is powerful and effective.

1 Peter 1:22: Now that you have purified yourselves by obeying the truth so that you have **sincere love for each other, love one another deeply, from the heart**.

1 Peter 4:9: **Offer hospitality to one another** without grumbling.

1 Peter 5:5: In the same way, you who are younger, submit yourselves to your elders. All of you, clothe yourselves with **humility toward one another**, because, "God opposes the proud but shows favor to the humble."

1 John 1:7: But if we walk in the light, as he is in the light, **we have fellowship with one another**, and the blood of Jesus, his Son, purifies us from all sin.

1 John 3:11, 23: For this is the message you heard from the beginning: **We should love one another**. ... And this is his command: to believe in the name of his Son, Jesus Christ, and **to love one another** as he commanded us.

1 John 4:7, 12: Dear friends, **let us love one another**, for love comes from God. Everyone who loves has been born of God and knows God. ... No one has ever seen God; but **if we love one another**, God lives in us and his love is made complete in us.

Romans 15:5-7: May the God who gives endurance and encouragement give you the **same attitude of mind toward each other that Christ Jesus had**, so that with one mind and one voice you may glorify the God and Father of our Lord Jesus Christ. **Accept one another**, then, just as Christ accepted you, in order to bring praise to God.

1 Corinthians 1:10: I appeal to you, brothers and sisters, in the name of our Lord Jesus Christ, that all of you **agree with one another** in what you say and that there be **no divisions among you**, but that you be perfectly united in mind and thought.

2 Corinthians 13:11: Finally, brothers and sisters, rejoice! Strive for full restoration, **encourage one another, be of one mind, live in peace**. And the God of love and peace will be with you.

Ephesians 4:3: Make every effort to keep the **unity of the Spirit** through the bond of peace.

Colossians 3:14: And over all these virtues put on love, which **binds them all together in perfect unity**.

The Sixth Day (Friday): Family & Friends, Neighbors & Enemies

Romans 16:17-18: I urge you, brothers and sisters, to **watch out for those who cause divisions** and put obstacles in your way that are contrary to the teaching you have learned. Keep away from them. For such people are not serving our Lord Christ, but their own appetites. By smooth talk and flattery they deceive the minds of naive people.

LOVING GOD MORE THAN FAMILY

Luke 14:26: "If anyone comes to me and does not **hate father and mother, wife and children, brothers and sisters** – yes, even their own life – such a person cannot be my disciple.

Luke 21:16-19: **You will be betrayed even by parents, brothers and sisters, relatives and friends**, and they will put some of you to death. **Everyone will hate you because of me**. But not a hair of your head will perish. Stand firm, and you will win life. (See also Matthew 10:21.)

Mark 10:29-30: "Truly I tell you," Jesus replied, "**no one who has left home or brothers or sisters or mother or father or children or fields for me and the gospel** will fail to receive a hundred times as much in this present age: homes, brothers, sisters, mothers, children and fields – along with persecutions – and in the age to come eternal life. (See also Matthew 19:29; Luke 18:29.)

Exodus 32:26-29: So he stood at the entrance to the camp and said, "Whoever is for the LORD, come to me." And all the Levites rallied to him. Then he said to them, "This is what the LORD, the God of Israel, says: 'Each man strap a sword to his side. Go back and forth through the camp from one end to the other, each killing his brother and friend and neighbor.'" The Levites did as Moses commanded, and that day about three thousand of the people died. Then Moses said, "**You have been set apart to the LORD today, for you were against your own sons and brothers**, and he has blessed you this day."

Deuteronomy 33:8-11: About Levi he said: "Your Thummim and Urim belong to your faithful servant. You tested him at Massah; you contended with him at the waters of Meribah. **He said of his father and mother, 'I have no regard for them.' He did not recognize his brothers or acknowledge his own children, but he watched over your word and guarded your covenant**. He teaches your precepts to Jacob and your law to Israel. He offers incense before you and whole burnt offerings on your altar. Bless all his skills, LORD, and be pleased with the work of his hands. Strike down those who rise against him, his foes till they rise no more."

Micah 7:5-7: **Do not trust a neighbor; put no confidence in a friend. Even with the woman who lies in your embrace** guard the words of your lips. For a **son dishonors his father, a daughter rises up against her mother, a daughter-in-law against her mother-in-law – a man's enemies are the members of his own household**. But as for me, I watch in hope for the LORD, I wait for God my Savior; my God will hear me.

Deuteronomy 13:6-10: **If your very own brother, or your son or daughter, or the wife you love, or your closest friend** secretly entices you, saying, "Let us go and worship other gods" (gods that neither you nor your ancestors have known, gods of the peoples around you, whether near or far, from one end of the land to the other), do not yield to them or listen to them. Show them no pity. Do not spare them or shield them. You must certainly put them to death. Your hand must be the first in putting them to death, and then the hands of all the people. Stone them to death, because they tried to turn you away from the LORD your God, who brought you out of Egypt, out of the land of slavery.

Jeremiah 9:4-6: "**Beware of your friends**; do not trust anyone in your clan. For every one of them is a deceiver, and every friend a slanderer. **Friend deceives friend**, and no one speaks the truth. They have taught their tongues to lie; they weary themselves with sinning. You live in the midst of deception; in their deceit they refuse to acknowledge me," declares the LORD.

Jeremiah 12:6: **Your relatives, members of your own family** – even they have betrayed you; they have raised a loud cry against you. Do not trust them, though they speak well of you.

FRIENDS

Matthew 11:19: The Son of Man came eating and drinking, and they say, 'Here is a glutton and a drunkard, a **friend of tax collectors and sinners**.' But wisdom is proved right by her deeds."

John 15:12-13: My command is this: Love each other as I have loved you. Greater love has no one than this: **to lay down one's life for one's friends**.

Proverbs 27:6: **Wounds from a friend** can be trusted, but an enemy multiplies kisses.

Proverbs 27:17: As iron sharpens iron, **so one person sharpens another**.

Proverbs 27:10: **Do not forsake your friend or a friend of your family**, and do not go to your relative's house when disaster strikes you – better a neighbor nearby than a relative far away.

Luke 16:9: I tell you, **use worldly wealth to gain friends for yourselves**, so that when it is gone, you will be welcomed into eternal dwellings.

Luke 14:12-14: Then Jesus said to his host, "When you give a luncheon or dinner, **do not invite your friends, your brothers or sisters, your relatives, or your rich neighbors**; if you do, they may invite you back and so you will be repaid. But when you give a banquet, **invite the poor, the crippled, the lame, the blind, and you will be blessed**. Although they cannot repay you, you will be repaid at the resurrection of the righteous."

The Sixth Day (Friday): Family & Friends, Neighbors & Enemies

Proverbs 12:26: **The righteous choose their friends carefully**, but the way of the wicked leads them astray.

Proverbs 17:17: A **friend** loves at all times, and a **brother** is born for a time of adversity.

Ecclesiastes 4:9-12: **Two are better than one**, because they have a good return for their labor: If either of them falls down, one can help the other up. But pity anyone who falls and has no one to help them up. Also, if two lie down together, they will keep warm. But how can one keep warm alone? Though one may be overpowered, two can defend themselves. **A cord of three strands is not quickly broken.**

Proverbs 18:24: One who has **unreliable friends** soon comes to ruin, but there is **a friend who sticks closer than a brother.**

Proverbs 27:9: Perfume and incense bring joy to the heart, and the **pleasantness of a friend** springs from their heartfelt advice.

Proverbs 17:9: Whoever would foster love covers over an offense, but whoever repeats the matter **separates close friends.**

1 Corinthians 15:33: Do not be misled: "**Bad company corrupts good character.**"

Proverbs 22:24-25: **Do not make friends with a hot-tempered person**, do not associate with one easily angered, or you may learn their ways and get yourself ensnared.

Job 6:14-17: Anyone who **withholds kindness from a friend forsakes the fear of the Almighty.** But my brothers are as undependable as intermittent streams, as the streams that overflow when darkened by thawing ice and swollen with melting snow, but that stop flowing in the dry season, and in the heat vanish from their channels.

NEIGHBORS

Romans 13:10: **Love does no harm to a neighbor.** Therefore love is the fulfillment of the law.

Leviticus 19:17-18: Do not hate a fellow Israelite in your heart. **Rebuke your neighbor frankly so you will not share in their guilt.** Do not seek revenge or bear a grudge against anyone among your people, but **love your neighbor as yourself.** I am the LORD.

Exodus 20:16: You shall not give false testimony **against your neighbor.**

Exodus 20:17: **You shall not covet your neighbor's house.** You shall not covet **your neighbor's wife**, or his male or female servant, his ox or donkey, or **anything that belongs to your neighbor.**

Leviticus 19:13: Do not defraud or rob **your neighbor.**

Psalm 101:5: Whoever **slanders their neighbor** in secret, I will put to silence; whoever has haughty eyes and a proud heart, I will not tolerate.

Proverbs 3:28: Do not say **to your neighbor**, "Come back tomorrow and I'll give it to you"-- when you already have it with you.

Proverbs 3:29: **Do not plot harm against your neighbor**, who lives trustfully near you.

Proverbs 11:12: **Whoever derides their neighbor has no sense**, but the one who has understanding holds their tongue.

Proverbs 14:21: **It is a sin to despise one's neighbor**, but blessed is the one who is kind to the needy.

Proverbs 16:29: A violent person **entices their neighbor** and leads them down a path that is not good.

Proverbs 24:28-29: **Do not testify against your neighbor** without cause--would you use your lips to mislead? Do not say, "I'll do to them as they have done to me; I'll pay them back for what they did."

Proverbs 25:7b-8: What you have seen with your eyes do not bring hastily to court, for what will you do in the end if **your neighbor** puts you to shame?

Proverbs 25:9-10: If you take **your neighbor** to court, do not betray another's confidence, or the one who hears it may shame you and the charge against you will stand.

Proverbs 25:17: **Seldom set foot in your neighbor's house**--too much of you, and they will hate you.

Proverbs 25:18: Like a club or a sword or a sharp arrow is one who gives **false testimony against a neighbor**.

Matthew 22:36-40: "Teacher, which is the greatest commandment in the Law?" Jesus replied: " 'Love the Lord your God with all your heart and with all your soul and with all your mind.' This is the first and greatest commandment. **And the second is like it: 'Love your neighbor as yourself.**' All the Law and the Prophets hang on these two commandments."

Mark 12:29-33: "The most important one," answered Jesus, "is this: 'Hear, O Israel: The Lord our God, the Lord is one. Love the Lord your God with all your heart and with all your soul and with all your mind and with all your strength.' **The second is this: 'Love your neighbor as yourself.**' There is no commandment greater than these." "Well said, teacher," the man replied. "You are right in saying that God is one and there is no other but him. To love him with all your heart, with all your understanding and with all your strength, **and to love your neighbor as yourself is more important than all burnt offerings and sacrifices.**"

The Sixth Day (Friday): Family & Friends, Neighbors & Enemies

Ephesians 4:25: Therefore each of you must put off falsehood and **speak truthfully to your neighbor**, for we are all members of one body.

Parable of the Good Samaritan:
Luke 10:25-37: On one occasion an expert in the law stood up to test Jesus. "Teacher," he asked, "what must I do to inherit eternal life?" "What is written in the Law?" he replied. "How do you read it?" He answered, " 'Love the Lord your God with all your heart and with all your soul and with all your strength and with all your mind'; and, **'Love your neighbor as yourself.'** "You have answered correctly," Jesus replied. "Do this and you will live." But he wanted to justify himself, so he asked Jesus, "**And who is my neighbor?**" In reply Jesus said: "A man was going down from Jerusalem to Jericho, when he was attacked by robbers. They stripped him of his clothes, beat him and went away, leaving him half dead. A priest happened to be going down the same road, and when he saw the man, he passed by on the other side. So too, a Levite, when he came to the place and saw him, passed by on the other side. But a Samaritan, as he traveled, came where the man was; and when he saw him, he took pity on him. He went to him and bandaged his wounds, pouring on oil and wine. Then he put the man on his own donkey, brought him to an inn and took care of him. The next day he took out two denarii and gave them to the innkeeper. 'Look after him,' he said, 'and when I return, I will reimburse you for any extra expense you may have.' "**Which of these three do you think was a neighbor to the man who fell into the hands of robbers?" The expert in the law replied, "The one who had mercy on him." Jesus told him, "Go and do likewise."**

James 2:8-13: If you really keep the royal law found in Scripture, "**Love your neighbor as yourself**," you are doing right. But if you show favoritism, you sin and are convicted by the law as lawbreakers. For whoever keeps the whole law and yet stumbles at just one point is guilty of breaking all of it. For he who said, "You shall not commit adultery," also said, "You shall not murder." If you do not commit adultery but do commit murder, you have become a lawbreaker. Speak and act as those who are going to be judged by the law that gives freedom, because judgment without mercy will be shown to anyone who has not been merciful. Mercy triumphs over judgment.

James 4:12: There is only one Lawgiver and Judge, the one who is able to save and destroy. **But you--who are you to judge your neighbor?**

ENEMIES

Matthew 5:43-48: "You have heard that it was said, 'Love your neighbor and hate your enemy.' **But I tell you, love your enemies and pray for those who persecute you**, that you may be children of your Father in heaven. He causes his sun to rise on the evil and the good, and sends rain on the righteous and the unrighteous. **If you love those who love you, what reward will you get?** Are not even the tax collectors doing that? **And if you greet only your own people, what are you doing more than others?** Do not even pagans do that? Be perfect, therefore, as your heavenly Father is perfect.

Romans 5:8-10: But God demonstrates his own love for us in this: **While we were still sinners, Christ died for us**. Since we have now been justified by his blood, how much more shall we be saved from God's wrath through him! For if, **while we were God's enemies, we were reconciled to him through the death of his Son**, how much more, having been reconciled, shall we be saved through his life!

Romans 12:19-21: Do not take revenge, my dear friends, but leave room for God's wrath, for it is written: "It is mine to avenge; I will repay," says the Lord. On the contrary: "**If your enemy is hungry, feed him; if he is thirsty, give him something to drink**. In doing this, you will heap burning coals on his head." **Do not be overcome by evil, but overcome evil with good.**

Matthew 7:12: So in everything, **do to others what you would have them do to you,** for this sums up the Law and the Prophets.

The Seventh Day (Saturday)
REST & REMEMBER

INDEX OF TOPICS:
- Song for the Sabbath
- Rest Scriptures
- Old Testament Sabbath Scriptures
- New Testament Sabbath Scriptures
- Remember Scriptures

SONG FOR THE SABBATH

Psalm 92:
A psalm. A song. **For the Sabbath day.**

It is good to praise the LORD and make music to your name, O Most High, proclaiming your love in the morning and your faithfulness at night, to the music of the ten-stringed lyre and the melody of the harp. For you make me glad by your deeds, LORD; I sing for joy at what your hands have done. How great are your works, LORD, how profound your thoughts!

Senseless people do not know, fools do not understand, that though the wicked spring up like grass and all evildoers flourish, they will be destroyed forever. But you, LORD, are forever exalted. For surely your enemies, LORD, surely your enemies will perish; all evildoers will be scattered. You have exalted my horn like that of a wild ox; fine oils have been poured on me. My eyes have seen the defeat of my adversaries; my ears have heard the rout of my wicked foes.

The righteous will flourish like a palm tree, they will grow like a cedar of Lebanon; planted in the house of the LORD, they will flourish in the courts of our God. They will still bear fruit in old age, they will stay fresh and green, proclaiming, "The LORD is upright; he is my Rock, and there is no wickedness in him."

REST SCRIPTURES

Matthew 11:28-30: "Come to me, all you who are weary and burdened, and **I will give you rest**. Take my yoke upon you and learn from me, for I am gentle and humble in heart, and **you will find rest for your souls**. For my yoke is easy and my burden is light."

Isaiah 55:1-3: "Come, all you who are thirsty, come to the waters; and you who have no money, come, buy and eat! Come, buy wine and milk without money and without cost. **Why spend money on what is not bread, and your labor on what does not satisfy?** Listen, listen to me, and eat what is good, and you will delight in the richest of fare. Give ear and come to me; listen, that you may live. I will make an everlasting covenant with you, my faithful love promised to David.

Exodus 33:14: The LORD replied, "My Presence will go with you, and **I will give you rest**."

Romans 4:3-8: What does Scripture say? "Abraham believed God, and it was credited to him as righteousness." Now to the one who works, wages are not credited as a gift but as an obligation. However, **to the one who does not work but trusts God who justifies the ungodly**, their faith is credited as righteousness. David says the same thing when he speaks of the blessedness of the one to whom God credits righteousness apart from works: "Blessed are those whose transgressions are forgiven, whose sins are covered. Blessed is the one whose sin the Lord will never count against them."

Hebrews 4:1-11: Therefore, since **the promise of entering his rest still stands**, let us be careful that none of you be found to have fallen short of it. For we also have had the good news proclaimed to us, just as they did; but the message they heard was of no value to them, because they did not share the faith of those who obeyed. Now we who have believed **enter that rest**, just as God has said, "So I declared on oath in my anger, 'They shall never enter my rest.'" And yet his works have been finished since the creation of the world. For somewhere he has spoken about the seventh day in these words: "**On the seventh day God rested from all his works**." And again in the passage above he says, "They shall never enter my rest." **Therefore since it still remains for some to enter that rest**, and since those who formerly had the good news proclaimed to them did not go in because of their disobedience, God again set a certain day, calling it "Today." This he did when a long time later he spoke through David, as in the passage already quoted: "Today, if you hear his voice, do not harden your hearts." For if Joshua had given them rest, God would not have spoken later about another day. **There remains, then, a Sabbath-rest for the people of God; for anyone who enters God's rest also rests from their works, just as God did from his. Let us, therefore, make every effort to enter that rest**, so that no one will perish by following their example of disobedience.

Deuteronomy 12:10: But you will cross the Jordan and settle in the land the LORD your God is giving you as an inheritance, and **he will give you rest** from all your enemies around you so that you will live in safety.

Exodus 14:14: The LORD will fight for you; **you need only to be still [rest]**.

Psalm 46:10: He says, "**Be still [rest]**, and know that I am God; I will be exalted among the nations, I will be exalted in the earth."

Psalm 91:1: Whoever dwells in the shelter of the Most High will **rest** in the shadow of the Almighty.

The Seventh Day (Saturday): Rest & Remember

Psalm 16:9-11: Therefore my heart is glad and my tongue rejoices; **my body also will rest secure**, because you will not abandon me to the realm of the dead, nor will you let your faithful one see decay. You make known to me the path of life; you will fill me with joy in your presence, with eternal pleasures at your right hand.

Psalm 62:1-5: **Truly my soul finds rest in God**; my salvation comes from him. Truly he is my rock and my salvation; he is my fortress, I will never be shaken. How long will you assault me? Would all of you throw me down – this leaning wall, this tottering fence? Surely they intend to topple me from my lofty place; they take delight in lies. With their mouths they bless, but in their hearts they curse. **Yes, my soul, find rest in God**; my hope comes from him.

Psalm 116:7-9: **Return to your rest, my soul**, for the LORD has been good to you. For you, LORD, have delivered me from death, my eyes from tears, my feet from stumbling, that I may walk before the LORD in the land of the living.

Psalm 127:1-2: Unless the LORD builds the house, the builders labor in vain. Unless the LORD watches over the city, the guards stand watch in vain. In vain you rise early and stay up late, toiling for food to eat – **for he grants sleep to those he loves**.

Isaiah 30:15: This is what the Sovereign LORD, the Holy One of Israel, says: "**In repentance and rest is your salvation**, in quietness and trust is your strength, but you would have none of it."

Isaiah 32:18: My people will live in peaceful dwelling places, in secure homes, **in undisturbed places of rest**.

Isaiah 57:2, 20: Those who walk uprightly enter into peace; they **find rest as they lie in death**. ... But the wicked are like the tossing sea, which cannot rest, whose waves cast up mire and mud.

Isaiah 28:11-12: Very well then, with foreign lips and strange tongues God will speak to this people, to whom he said, "**This is the resting place, let the weary rest**"; and, "**This is the place of repose**" – but they would not listen.

Jeremiah 6:16: This is what the LORD says: "Stand at the crossroads and look; ask for the ancient paths, ask where the good way is, and walk in it, and **you will find rest for your souls**. But you said, 'We will not walk in it.'

1 John 3:19: This is how we know that we belong to the truth and how **we set our hearts at rest in his presence**:

Mark 6:31-32: Then, because so many people were coming and going that they did not even have a chance to eat, he said to them, "**Come with me by yourselves to a quiet place and get some rest**." So they went away by themselves in a boat to a solitary place. (See also Matthew 14:13, 23; Mark 1:35; Luke 4:42, 5:16, 6:12, 9:10.)

Genesis 2:21: So the LORD God **caused the man to fall into a deep sleep**; and while he was sleeping, he took one of the man's ribs and then closed up the place with flesh.

Genesis 15:12, 18: As the sun was setting, **Abram fell into a deep sleep**, and a thick and dreadful darkness came over him. ... On that day the LORD made a covenant with Abram and said, "To your descendants I give this land, from the Wadi of Egypt to the great river, the Euphrates—

Daniel 10:7-9: I, Daniel, was the only one who saw the vision; those who were with me did not see it, but such terror overwhelmed them that they fled and hid themselves. So I was left alone, gazing at this great vision; I had no strength left, my face turned deathly pale and I was helpless. Then I heard him speaking, and as I listened to him, **I fell into a deep sleep**, my face to the ground.

Daniel 8:27: I, Daniel, was worn out. **I lay exhausted for several days**. Then I got up and went about the king's business. I was appalled by the vision; it was beyond understanding.

OLD TESTAMENT SABBATH - THE SEVENTH DAY

Genesis 2:2-3: By the seventh day God had finished the work he had been doing; so **on the seventh day he rested** from all his work. Then **God blessed the seventh day and made it holy**, because on it **he rested from all the work of creating** that he had done.

Exodus 16:4-5, 22-30: Then the LORD said to Moses, "I will rain down bread from heaven for you. The people are to go out each day and gather enough for that day. In this way I will test them and see whether they will follow my instructions. On the sixth day they are to prepare what they bring in, and that is to be twice as much as they gather on the other days." ... On the sixth day, they gathered twice as much – two omers for each person – and the leaders of the community came and reported this to Moses. He said to them, "This is what the LORD commanded: **'Tomorrow is to be a day of sabbath rest, a holy sabbath to the LORD**. So bake what you want to bake and boil what you want to boil. Save whatever is left and keep it until morning.'" So they saved it until morning, as Moses commanded, and it did not stink or get maggots in it. "Eat it today," Moses said, "because **today is a sabbath to the LORD**. You will not find any of it on the ground today. Six days you are to gather it, but on the seventh day, the Sabbath, there will not be any." Nevertheless, some of the people went out on the seventh day to gather it, but they found none. Then the LORD said to Moses, "How long will you refuse to keep my commands and my instructions? Bear in mind that **the LORD has given you the Sabbath**; that is why on the sixth day he gives you bread for two days. **Everyone is to stay where they are on the seventh day; no one is to go out.**" So the people rested on the seventh day.

Exodus 20:8-11: [4th Commandment] "**Remember the Sabbath day by keeping it holy.** Six days you shall labor and do all your work, but **the seventh day is a sabbath to the LORD your God**. On it you shall **not do any work**, neither you, nor your son or daughter, nor your male or female servant, nor your animals, nor any foreigner residing in your towns. For in six days

The Seventh Day (Saturday): Rest & Remember

the LORD made the heavens and the earth, the sea, and all that is in them, but **he rested on the seventh day. Therefore the LORD blessed the Sabbath day and made it holy.**

Exodus 31:13-17: "Say to the Israelites, **'You must observe my Sabbaths**. This will be a sign between me and you for the generations to come, so you may know that I am the LORD, who makes you holy. **'Observe the Sabbath, because it is holy to you**. Anyone who desecrates it is to be put to death; those who do any work on that day must be cut off from their people. For six days work is to be done, but **the seventh day is a day of sabbath rest, holy to the LORD**. Whoever does any work on the Sabbath day is to be put to death. **The Israelites are to observe the Sabbath**, celebrating it for the generations to come as a lasting covenant. It will be a sign between me and the Israelites forever, for **in six days the LORD made the heavens and the earth, and on the seventh day he rested and was refreshed.**'"

Isaiah 58:13-14: "If you **keep your feet from breaking the Sabbath and from doing as you please on my holy day, if you call the Sabbath a delight and the LORD's holy day honorable, and if you honor it by not going your own way and not doing as you please or speaking idle words**, then you will find your joy in the LORD, and I will cause you to ride in triumph on the heights of the land and to feast on the inheritance of your father Jacob." The mouth of the LORD has spoken.

Ezekiel 20:9-13: But for the sake of my name, I brought them out of Egypt. I did it to keep my name from being profaned in the eyes of the nations among whom they lived and in whose sight I had revealed myself to the Israelites. Therefore I led them out of Egypt and brought them into the wilderness. I gave them my decrees and made known to them my laws, by which the person who obeys them will live. Also **I gave them my Sabbaths as a sign between us, so they would know that I the LORD made them holy**. Yet the people of Israel rebelled against me in the wilderness. They did not follow my decrees but rejected my laws – by which the person who obeys them will live – and they utterly desecrated **my Sabbaths**. So I said I would pour out my wrath on them and destroy them in the wilderness.

Leviticus 23:3: "'There are six days when you may work, but **the seventh day is a day of sabbath rest**, a day of sacred assembly. **You are not to do any work**; wherever you live, it is **a sabbath to the LORD**.

1 Chronicles 23:30-31: They were also to stand every morning to thank and praise the LORD. They were to do the same in the evening and whenever burnt offerings were presented to the LORD on **the Sabbaths**, at the New Moon feasts and at the appointed festivals. They were to serve before the LORD regularly in the proper number and in the way prescribed for them.

Isaiah 1:13-17: Stop bringing meaningless offerings! Your incense is detestable to me. New Moons, **Sabbaths** and convocations – I cannot bear your worthless assemblies. Your New Moon feasts and your appointed festivals I hate with all my being. They have become a burden to me; I am weary of bearing them. When you spread out your hands in prayer, I hide my eyes from you; even when you offer many prayers, I am not listening. Your hands are full of blood! Wash and make yourselves clean. Take your evil deeds out of my sight; stop doing wrong. Learn to do right; seek justice. Defend the oppressed. Take up the cause of the fatherless; plead the case of the widow.

Isaiah 56:1-7: This is what the LORD says: "Maintain justice and do what is right, for my salvation is close at hand and my righteousness will soon be revealed. Blessed is the one who does this – the person who holds it fast, **who keeps the Sabbath without desecrating it**, and keeps their hands from doing any evil." Let no foreigner who is bound to the LORD say, "The LORD will surely exclude me from his people." And let no eunuch complain, "I am only a dry tree." For this is what the LORD says: "To the eunuchs **who keep my Sabbaths**, who choose what pleases me and hold fast to my covenant – to them I will give within my temple and its walls a memorial and a name better than sons and daughters; I will give them an everlasting name that will endure forever. And foreigners who bind themselves to the LORD to minister to him, to love the name of the LORD, and to be his servants, all who keep the Sabbath without desecrating it and who hold fast to my covenant – these I will bring to my holy mountain and give them joy in my house of prayer. Their burnt offerings and sacrifices will be accepted on my altar; for my house will be called a house of prayer for all nations."

Leviticus 25:2-7: "Speak to the Israelites and say to them: 'When you enter the land I am going to give you, **the land itself must observe a sabbath to the LORD**. For six years sow your fields, and for six years prune your vineyards and gather their crops. **But in the seventh year the land is to have a year of sabbath rest, a sabbath to the LORD**. Do not sow your fields or prune your vineyards. Do not reap what grows of itself or harvest the grapes of your untended vines. **The land is to have a year of rest**. Whatever the land yields during the sabbath year will be food for you – for yourself, your male and female servants, and the hired worker and temporary resident who live among you, as well as for your livestock and the wild animals in your land. Whatever the land produces may be eaten.

NEW TESTAMENT SABBATH – REST IN CHRIST

Colossians 2:16-17: Therefore do not let anyone judge you by what you eat or drink, or with regard to a religious festival, a New Moon celebration or **a Sabbath day**. These are a shadow of the things that were to come; the reality, however, is found in Christ.

Romans 14:4-8: Who are you to judge someone else's servant? To their own master, servants stand or fall. And they will stand, for the Lord is able to make them stand. One person considers one **day more sacred than another**; another considers every day alike. Each of them should be fully convinced in their own mind. Whoever regards one day as special does so to the Lord. Whoever eats meat does so to the Lord, for they give thanks to God; and whoever abstains does so to the Lord and gives thanks to God. For none of us lives for ourselves alone, and none of us dies for ourselves alone. If we live, we live for the Lord; and if we die, we die for the Lord. So, whether we live or die, we belong to the Lord.

The Seventh Day (Saturday): Rest & Remember

Galatians 4:9-11: But now that you know God – or rather are known by God – how is it that you are turning back to those weak and miserable forces? Do you wish to be enslaved by them all over again? You are **observing special days** and months and seasons and years! I fear for you, that somehow I have wasted my efforts on you.

John 5:8-11, 16-18: Then Jesus said to him, "Get up! Pick up your mat and walk." At once the man was cured; he picked up his mat and walked. **The day on which this took place was a Sabbath**, and so the Jewish leaders said to the man who had been healed, "It is the Sabbath; the law forbids you to carry your mat." But he replied, "The man who made me well said to me, 'Pick up your mat and walk.'" ... So, because Jesus was doing these things on the Sabbath, the Jewish leaders began to persecute him. In his defense Jesus said to them, "**My Father is always at his work to this very day, and I too am working.**" For this reason they tried all the more to kill him; **not only was he breaking the Sabbath**, but he was even calling God his own Father, making himself equal with God.

John 7:21-24: Jesus said to them, "I did one miracle, and you are all amazed. Yet, because Moses gave you circumcision (though actually it did not come from Moses, but from the patriarchs), you circumcise a boy on the Sabbath. Now if a boy can be **circumcised on the Sabbath** so that the law of Moses may not be broken, why are you angry with me for **healing a man's whole body on the Sabbath**? Stop judging by mere appearances, but instead judge correctly."

Matthew 12:1-12: At that time Jesus went through the grainfields on the Sabbath. His disciples were hungry and began to pick some heads of grain and eat them. When the Pharisees saw this, they said to him, "Look! Your disciples are doing what is unlawful on the Sabbath." He answered, "Haven't you read what David did when he and his companions were hungry? He entered the house of God, and he and his companions ate the consecrated bread – which was not lawful for them to do, but only for the priests. Or haven't you read in the Law that the priests on Sabbath duty in the temple desecrate the Sabbath and yet are innocent? I tell you that something greater than the temple is here. If you had known what these words mean, 'I desire mercy, not sacrifice,' you would not have condemned the innocent. **For the Son of Man is Lord of the Sabbath.**" Going on from that place, he went into their synagogue, and a man with a shriveled hand was there. Looking for a reason to bring charges against Jesus, they asked him, "**Is it lawful to heal on the Sabbath**?" He said to them, "**If any of you has a sheep and it falls into a pit on the Sabbath**, will you not take hold of it and lift it out? How much more valuable is a person than a sheep! **Therefore it is lawful to do good on the Sabbath.**" (See also Mark 2; Luke 6, 13:10-16.)

Mark 2:27: Then he said to them, "**The Sabbath was made for man, not man for the Sabbath.**

Mark 3:1-5: Another time Jesus went into the synagogue, and a man with a shriveled hand was there. Some of them were looking for a reason to accuse Jesus, so they watched him closely to see **if he would heal him on the Sabbath**. Jesus said to the man with the shriveled hand, "Stand up in front of everyone." Then Jesus asked them, "Which is lawful on the Sabbath: to do good or to do evil, to save life or to kill?" But they remained silent. He looked around at them in anger and, deeply distressed at their stubborn hearts, said to the man, "Stretch out your hand." He stretched it out, and his hand was completely restored.

Luke 4:16, 31: He went to Nazareth, where he had been brought up, and **on the Sabbath day** he went into the synagogue, as was his custom. He stood up to read, ... Then he went down to Capernaum, a town in Galilee, and **on the Sabbath he taught the people**. (See also Mark 1:21, 6:2.)

Acts 17:2-3: As was his custom, Paul went into the synagogue, and **on three Sabbath days he reasoned with them from the Scriptures**, explaining and proving that the Messiah had to suffer and rise from the dead. "This Jesus I am proclaiming to you is the Messiah," he said. (See also Acts 13:14-16, 27, 42, 44, 16:13, 18:4.)

Matthew 24:20: Pray that your flight will not take place in winter or **on the Sabbath**.

Revelation 14:11, 13: And the smoke of their torment will rise for ever and ever. There will be **no rest day or night for those who worship the beast and its image**, or for anyone who receives the mark of its name." ... Then I heard a voice from heaven say, "Write this: Blessed are the dead who die in the Lord from now on." "Yes," says the Spirit, "they will rest from their labor, for their deeds will follow them."

REMEMBER SCRIPTURES

Deuteronomy 5:15: **Remember** that you were slaves in Egypt and that the LORD your God brought you out of there with a mighty hand and an outstretched arm. Therefore the LORD your God has commanded you to **observe the Sabbath day**. (See also Deuteronomy 16:12, 24:18, 22.)

Deuteronomy 4:10: **Remember** the day you stood before the LORD your God at Horeb, when he said to me, "Assemble the people before me to hear my words so that they may learn to revere me as long as they live in the land and may teach them to their children."

Deuteronomy 7:18: But do not be afraid of them; **remember well** what the LORD your God did to Pharaoh and to all Egypt.

Deuteronomy 8:2: **Remember** how the LORD your God led you all the way in the wilderness these forty years, to humble and test you in order to know what was in your heart, whether or not you would keep his commands.

Deuteronomy 8:18: But **remember** the LORD your God, for it is he who gives you the ability to produce wealth, and so confirms his covenant, which he swore to your ancestors, as it is today.

2 Timothy 2:8: **Remember** Jesus Christ, raised from the dead, descended from David. This is my gospel,

The Seventh Day (Saturday): Rest & Remember

Revelation 3:3: **Remember**, therefore, what you have received and heard; hold it fast, and repent. But if you do not wake up, I will come like a thief, and you will not know at what time I will come to you.

Matthew 16:9: Do you still not understand? Don't you **remember** the five loaves for the five thousand, and how many basketfuls you gathered?

Psalm 105:4-7: Look to the LORD and his strength; seek his face always. **Remember** the wonders he has done, his miracles, and the judgments he pronounced, you his servants, the descendants of Abraham, his chosen ones, the children of Jacob. He is the LORD our God; his judgments are in all the earth.

Psalm 77:3-6, 11-14: **I remembered you, God**, and I groaned; I meditated, and my spirit grew faint. You kept my eyes from closing; I was too troubled to speak. I thought about the former days, the years of long ago; **I remembered** my songs in the night. My heart meditated and my spirit asked: ... **I will remember** the deeds of the LORD; yes, **I will remember** your miracles of long ago. I will consider all your works and meditate on all your mighty deeds." Your ways, God, are holy. What god is as great as our God? You are the God who performs miracles; you display your power among the peoples.

Hebrews 10:32-35: **Remember** those earlier days after you had received the light, when you endured in a great conflict full of suffering. Sometimes you were publicly exposed to insult and persecution; at other times you stood side by side with those who were so treated. You suffered along with those in prison and joyfully accepted the confiscation of your property, because you knew that you yourselves had better and lasting possessions. So do not throw away your confidence; it will be richly rewarded.

Ephesians 2:11-13: Therefore, **remember** that formerly you who are Gentiles by birth and called "uncircumcised" by those who call themselves "the circumcision" (which is done in the body by human hands) – **remember** that at that time you were separate from Christ, excluded from citizenship in Israel and foreigners to the covenants of the promise, without hope and without God in the world. But now in Christ Jesus you who once were far away have been brought near by the blood of Christ.

Psalm 22:27-28: All the ends of the earth will **remember** and turn to the LORD, and all the families of the nations will bow down before him, for dominion belongs to the LORD and he rules over the nations.

Deuteronomy 32:7: **Remember the days of old**; consider the generations long past. Ask your father and he will tell you, your elders, and they will explain to you.

Psalm 143:5: **I remember the days of long ago**; I meditate on all your works and consider what your hands have done.

Isaiah 46:9: **Remember the former things**, those of long ago; I am God, and there is no other; I am God, and there is none like me.

Psalm 119:52, 55: **I remember, LORD, your ancient laws**, and I find comfort in them. ... In the night, LORD, I remember your name, that I may keep your law.

Jonah 2:7: "When my life was ebbing away, **I remembered you, LORD,** and my prayer rose to you, to your holy temple.

Psalm 78:42-43: **They did not remember** his power – the day he redeemed them from the oppressor, the day he displayed his signs in Egypt, his wonders in the region of Zoan.

Ezekiel 16:22, 43, 60-61, 63: In all your detestable practices and your prostitution **you did not remember the days of your youth**, when you were naked and bare, kicking about in your blood. ... "'Because **you did not remember** the days of your youth but enraged me with all these things, I will surely bring down on your head what you have done, declares the Sovereign LORD. Did you not add lewdness to all your other detestable practices? ... Yet I will remember the covenant I made with you in the days of your youth, and I will establish an everlasting covenant with you. **Then you will remember** your ways and be ashamed when you receive your sisters, both those who are older than you and those who are younger. I will give them to you as daughters, but not on the basis of my covenant with you. ... Then, when I make atonement for you for all you have done, **you will remember** and be ashamed and never again open your mouth because of your humiliation, declares the Sovereign LORD.'"

Psalm 137:6: May my tongue cling to the roof of my mouth **if I do not remember you**, if I do not consider Jerusalem my highest joy.

Deuteronomy 9:7: **Remember this and never forget** how you aroused the anger of the LORD your God in the wilderness. From the day you left Egypt until you arrived here, you have been rebellious against the LORD.

Every Day
THE KINGDOM OF GOD

INDEX OF TOPICS:
- Receiving the Kingdom of God
- Messiah's Eternal Kingdom
- Preaching the Kingdom of God
- Kingdom Parables
- Who Will and Will Not Enter the Kingdom of God

RECEIVING THE KINGDOM OF GOD

Matthew 6:9-13: "This, then, is how you should pray: 'Our Father in heaven, hallowed be your name, **your kingdom come**, your will be done, on earth as it is in heaven. Give us today our daily bread. And forgive us our debts, as we also have forgiven our debtors. And lead us not into temptation, but deliver us from the evil one.'

Matthew 6:33-34: But **seek first his kingdom** and his righteousness, and all these things will be given to you as well.

Matthew 16:19: I will give you the **keys of the kingdom of heaven**; whatever you bind on earth will be bound in heaven, and whatever you loose on earth will be loosed in heaven."

Luke 12:32: "Do not be afraid, little flock, for your Father has been pleased to **give you the kingdom**.

Luke 17:20-21: Once, on being asked by the Pharisees when the **kingdom of God** would come, Jesus replied, "**The coming of the kingdom of God is not something that can be observed**, nor will people say, 'Here it is,' or 'There it is,' because **the kingdom of God is in your midst**."

1 Peter 2:9-10: But you are a **chosen people, a royal priesthood, a holy nation, God's special possession**, that you may declare the praises of him who called you out of darkness into his wonderful light. Once you were not a people, but now you are the people of God; once you had not received mercy, but now you have received mercy.

Revelation 1:5b-6: To him who loves us and has freed us from our sins by his blood, and **has made us to be a kingdom and priests** to serve his God and Father – to him be glory and power for ever and ever! Amen.

Revelation 5:10: You have **made them to be a kingdom and priests** to serve our God, and they will reign on the earth."

Luke 18:29-30: "Truly I tell you," Jesus said to them, "no one who has left home or wife or brothers or sisters or parents or children **for the sake of the kingdom of God** will fail to receive many times as much in this age, and in the age to come eternal life." (See also Matthew 19:29; Mark 10:29-30.)

MESSIAH'S ETERNAL KINGDOM

John 18:36-37: Jesus said, "**My kingdom is not of this world.** If it were, my servants would fight to prevent my arrest by the Jewish leaders. But now **my kingdom is from another place.**" "You are a king, then!" said Pilate. Jesus answered, "You say that I am a king. In fact, the reason I was born and came into the world is to testify to the truth. Everyone on the side of truth listens to me."

Romans 14:17-18: For **the kingdom of God** is not a matter of eating and drinking, but of righteousness, peace and joy in the Holy Spirit, because anyone who serves Christ in this way is pleasing to God and receives human approval.

1 Corinthians 4:20: For **the kingdom of God** is not a matter of talk but of power.

Revelation 1:9: I, John, your brother and **companion in the suffering and kingdom and patient endurance that are ours in Jesus**, was on the island of Patmos because of the word of God and the testimony of Jesus.

Revelation 11:15: The seventh angel sounded his trumpet, and there were loud voices in heaven, which said: "**The kingdom of the world has become the kingdom of our Lord and of his Messiah**, and he will reign for ever and ever."

Revelation 12:10: Then I heard a loud voice in heaven say: "Now have come the salvation and the power and the **kingdom of our God, and the authority of his Messiah [King]**. For the accuser of our brothers and sisters, who accuses them before our God day and night, has been hurled down.

Mark 11:10: Blessed is the coming **kingdom of our father David!** Hosanna in the highest heaven!

Luke 1:32-33: He will be great and will be called the Son of the Most High. The Lord God will give him the **throne of his father David**, and he will reign over Jacob's descendants forever; **his kingdom will never end.**"

2 Samuel 7:12-16: When your days are over and you rest with your ancestors, I will raise up your offspring to succeed you, your own flesh and blood, and **I will establish his kingdom.** He is the one who will build a house for my Name, and **I will establish the throne of his**

kingdom forever. I will be his father, and he will be my son. When he does wrong, I will punish him with a rod wielded by men, with floggings inflicted by human hands. But my love will never be taken away from him, as I took it away from Saul, whom I removed from before you. **Your house and your kingdom will endure forever before me; your throne will be established forever."**

Isaiah 9:6-7: For to us a child is born, to us a son is given, and the **government** will be on his shoulders. And he will be called Wonderful Counselor, Mighty God, Everlasting Father, Prince of Peace. **Of the greatness of his government and peace there will be no end. He will reign on David's throne and over his kingdom**, establishing and upholding it with justice and righteousness from that time on and forever. The zeal of the LORD Almighty will accomplish this.

Genesis 49:10-12: The **scepter** will not depart from Judah, nor the **ruler's staff** from between his feet, until he to whom it belongs shall come and the obedience of the nations shall be his. He will tether his donkey to a vine, his colt to the choicest branch; he will wash his garments in wine, his robes in the blood of grapes. His eyes will be darker than wine, his teeth whiter than milk.

Revelation 5:5: Then one of the elders said to me, "Do not weep! See, the **Lion [King] of the tribe of Judah**, the Root of David, has triumphed. He is able to open the scroll and its seven seals."

Hebrews 1:8-9: But about the Son he says, "**Your throne, O God, will last for ever and ever; a scepter of justice will be the scepter of your kingdom**. You have loved righteousness and hated wickedness; therefore God, your God, has set you above your companions by anointing you with the oil of joy." (Quoting Psalm 45:6-7.)

Acts 1:3, 6-7: After his suffering, he presented himself to them and gave many convincing proofs that he was alive. He appeared to them over a period of forty days and **spoke about the kingdom of God**... Then they gathered around him and asked him, "Lord, are you at this time going to **restore the kingdom to Israel?**" He said to them: "It is not for you to know the times or dates the Father has set by his own authority.

Zechariah 14:9: **The LORD will be king over the whole earth.** On that day there will be one LORD, and his name the only name.

1 Corinthians 15:22-26: For as in Adam all die, so in Christ all will be made alive. But each in turn: Christ, the firstfruits; then, when he comes, those who belong to him. Then the end will come, when he **hands over the kingdom to God the Father after he has destroyed all dominion, authority and power**. For he must reign until he has put all his enemies under his feet. The last enemy to be destroyed is death.

Revelation 15:2-4: And I saw what looked like a sea of glass glowing with fire and, standing beside the sea, those who had been victorious over the beast and its image and over the number of its name. They held harps given them by God and sang the song of God's servant Moses and of the Lamb: "Great and marvelous are your deeds, Lord God Almighty. Just and true are your ways, **King of the nations**. Who will not fear you, Lord, and bring glory to your name? For you alone are holy. All nations will come and worship before you, for your righteous acts have been revealed."

Psalm 103:19: The LORD has established **his throne** in heaven, and **his kingdom rules over all**.

Daniel 2:44: "In the time of those kings, **the God of heaven will set up a kingdom that will never be destroyed**, nor will it be left to another people. It will crush all those kingdoms and bring them to an end, but **it will itself endure forever**.

Daniel 4:2-3: It is my pleasure to tell you about the miraculous signs and wonders that the Most High God has performed for me. How great are his signs, how mighty his wonders! **His kingdom is an eternal kingdom; his dominion endures from generation to generation**.

Daniel 7:13-27: "In my vision at night I looked, and there before me was one like a son of man, coming with the clouds of heaven. He approached the Ancient of Days and was led into his presence. He was given **authority, glory and sovereign power**; all nations and peoples of every language worshiped him. **His dominion is an everlasting dominion that will not pass away, and his kingdom is one that will never be destroyed**. "I, Daniel, was troubled in spirit, and the visions that passed through my mind disturbed me. I approached one of those standing there and asked him the meaning of all this. "So he told me and gave me the interpretation of these things: 'The four great beasts are four kings that will rise from the earth. **But the holy people of the Most High will receive the kingdom and will possess it forever – yes, for ever and ever.**' "Then I wanted to know the meaning of the fourth beast, which was different from all the others and most terrifying, with its iron teeth and bronze claws – the beast that crushed and devoured its victims and trampled underfoot whatever was left. I also wanted to know about the ten horns on its head and about the other horn that came up, before which three of them fell – the horn that looked more imposing than the others and that had eyes and a mouth that spoke boastfully. As I watched, this horn was waging war against the holy people and defeating them, until the Ancient of Days came and pronounced **judgment in favor of the holy people of the Most High, and the time came when they possessed the kingdom**. "He gave me this explanation: 'The fourth beast is a fourth kingdom that will appear on earth. It will be different from all the other kingdoms and will devour the whole earth, trampling it down and crushing it. The ten horns are ten kings who will come from this kingdom. After them another king will arise, different from the earlier ones; he will subdue three kings. He will speak against the Most High and oppress his holy people and try to change the set times and the laws. The holy people will be delivered into his hands for a time, times and half a time." 'But the court will sit, and his power will be taken away and completely destroyed forever. **Then the sovereignty, power and greatness of all the kingdoms under heaven will be handed over to the holy people of the Most High. His kingdom will be an everlasting kingdom, and all rulers will worship and obey him.**'

Psalm 145:10-13: All your works praise you, LORD; your faithful people extol you. **They tell of the glory of your kingdom and speak of your might**, so that all people may know of your mighty acts and **the glorious splendor of your kingdom. Your kingdom is an everlasting kingdom, and your dominion endures through all generations**. The LORD is trustworthy in all he promises and faithful in all he does.

Revelation 21:3-7: And I heard a loud voice **from the throne saying, "Look! God's dwelling place is now among the people, and he will dwell with them.** They will be his people, and God himself will be with them and be their God. 'He will wipe every tear from their eyes. There will be no more death' or mourning or crying or pain, for the old order of things has passed away." He who was seated on the throne said, "I am making everything new!" Then he said, "Write this down, for these words are trustworthy and true." He said to me: "It is done. I am the Alpha and the Omega, the Beginning and the End. To the thirsty I will give water without cost from the spring of the water of life. Those who are victorious will inherit all this, and I will be their God and they will be my children.

PREACHING THE KINGDOM OF GOD

Matthew 4:17, 23: From that time on Jesus began to preach, "Repent, for the **kingdom of heaven** has come near." ... Jesus went throughout Galilee, teaching in their synagogues, **proclaiming the good news of the kingdom**, and healing every disease and sickness among the people.

Matthew 24:14: And **this gospel of the kingdom** will be preached in the whole world as a testimony to all nations, and then the end will come.

Luke 24:46-47: He told them, "This is what is written: The **Messiah [King]** will suffer and rise from the dead on the third day, and repentance for the forgiveness of sins will be preached in his name to all nations, beginning at Jerusalem.

Matthew 10:1, 7-8: Jesus called his twelve disciples to him and gave them authority to drive out impure spirits and to heal every disease and sickness ... As you go, proclaim this message: **'The kingdom of heaven** has come near.' Heal the sick, raise the dead, cleanse those who have leprosy, drive out demons. Freely you have received; freely give.

Luke 10:9: Heal the sick who are there and tell them, **'The kingdom of God has come near to you.'**

Luke 16:16: The Law and the Prophets were proclaimed until John. Since that time, **the good news of the kingdom of God** is being preached, and everyone is forcing their way into it.

Luke 9:57-62: As they were walking along the road, a man said to him, "I will follow you wherever you go." Jesus replied, "Foxes have dens and birds have nests, but the Son of Man has no place to lay his head." He said to another man, "Follow me." But he replied,

"Lord, first let me go and bury my father." Jesus said to him, "Let the dead bury their own dead, but **you go and proclaim the kingdom of God**." Still another said, "I will follow you, Lord; but first let me go back and say goodbye to my family." Jesus replied, "No one who puts a hand to the plow and looks back is fit for service in the kingdom of God."

2 Timothy 4:1-2: In the presence of God and of Christ Jesus, who will judge the living and the dead, and in view of his appearing and **his kingdom**, I give you this charge: Preach the word; be prepared in season and out of season; correct, rebuke and encourage – with great patience and careful instruction.

KINGDOM PARABLES

The Purpose of Parables – Matthew 13:10-17; Mark 4:10-12; Luke 8:9-10
He replied, "Because the knowledge of the **secrets of the kingdom of heaven** has been given to you, but not to them...

Matthew 13:52: He said to them, "Therefore every teacher of the law who has become **a disciple in the kingdom of heaven** is like the owner of a house who brings out of his storeroom new treasures as well as old."

Parable of the Soils/Sower – Matthew 13:1-9, 18-23; Mark 4:1-9, 13-20; Luke 8:4-8, 11-15
"Listen then to what the parable of the sower means: When anyone **hears the message about the kingdom**...

Parable of the Weeds – Matthew 13:24-30, 36-43; Mark 4:26-29
He answered, "The one who sowed the good seed is the Son of Man. The field is the world, and the **good seed stands for the people of the kingdom**...

Parable of the Mustard Seed – Matthew 13:31-32; Mark 4:30-32; Luke 13:18-19
Matthew 13:31-32: He told them another parable: "The **kingdom of heaven is like** a mustard seed, which a man took and planted in his field. Though it is the smallest of all seeds, yet when it grows, it is the largest of garden plants and becomes a tree, so that the birds come and perch in its branches."

Parable of Leaven – Matthew 13:33; Luke 13:20-21
Matthew 13:33: He told them still another parable: "**The kingdom of heaven is like** yeast that a woman took and mixed into about sixty pounds of flour until it worked all through the dough."

Parables of the Hidden Treasure & Fine Pearl –
Matthew 13:43-46: "**The kingdom of heaven is like** treasure hidden in a field. When a man found it, he hid it again, and then in his joy went and sold all he had and bought that field. Again, **the kingdom of heaven is like** a merchant looking for fine pearls. When he found one of great value, he went away and sold everything he had and bought it.

Parable of the Net –
Matthew 13:47-50: "Once again, **the kingdom of heaven is like** a net that was let down into the lake and caught all kinds of fish. When it was full, the fishermen pulled it up on the shore. Then they sat down and collected the good fish in baskets, but threw the bad away. This is how it will be at the end of the age. The angels will come and separate the wicked from the righteous and throw them into the blazing furnace, where there will be weeping and gnashing of teeth.

Parable of the Unforgiving Servant –
Matthew 18:23-35: "Therefore, **the kingdom of heaven is like** a king who wanted to settle accounts with his servants...

Parable of the Talents – Matthew 25:14-30; Luke 19:11-27
Luke 19:11-27: While they were listening to this, he went on to tell them a parable, because he was near Jerusalem and the **people thought that the kingdom of God was going to appear at once**. He said: "A man of noble birth went to a distant country to have himself appointed king and then to return. So he called ten of his servants and gave them ten minas. 'Put this money to work,' he said, 'until I come back.' ..."He replied, 'I tell you that to everyone who has, more will be given, but as for the one who has nothing, even what they have will be taken away. But those enemies of mine who did not want me to be king over them – bring them here and kill them in front of me.'"

Parable of the Landowner –
Matthew 20:1-16: "For **the kingdom of heaven is like** a landowner who went out early in the morning to hire workers for his vineyard. ... "So the last will be first, and the first will be last."

Parable of the Two Sons –
Matthew 21:28-32: "What do you think? There was a man who had two sons. He went to the first and said, 'Son, go and work today in the vineyard.' 'I will not,' he answered, but later he changed his mind and went. "Then the father went to the other son and said the same thing. He answered, 'I will, sir,' but he did not go. "Which of the two did what his father wanted?" "The first," they answered. Jesus said to them, "Truly I tell you, the **tax collectors and the prostitutes are entering the kingdom of God ahead of you**.

Parable of the Tenants – Matthew 21:33-43; Mark 12:-1-11; Luke 20:9-18
Matthew 21:33-43: "Listen to another parable: There was a landowner who planted a vineyard... "Therefore I tell you that **the kingdom of God** will be taken away from you and given to a people who will produce its fruit."

Parable of the Ten Bridesmaids –
Matthew 25:1-13: "**At that time the kingdom of heaven will be like** ten virgins who took their lamps and went out to meet the bridegroom. ... "Therefore keep watch, because you do not know the day or the hour.

WHO WILL AND WILL NOT ENTER THE KINGDOM OF GOD

Matthew 5:3, 10, 18-20: "Blessed are the poor in spirit, for **theirs is the kingdom of heaven**. ... Blessed are those who are persecuted because of righteousness, for **theirs is the kingdom of heaven**... For truly I tell you, until heaven and earth disappear, not the smallest letter, not the least stroke of a pen, will by any means disappear from the Law until everything is accomplished. Therefore anyone who sets aside one of the least of these commands and teaches others accordingly will be called **least in the kingdom of heaven**, but whoever practices and teaches these commands will be called **great in the kingdom of heaven**. For I tell you that unless your righteousness surpasses that of the Pharisees and the teachers of the law, **you will certainly not enter the kingdom of heaven**. (See also Luke 6.)

Matthew 7:21-23: "Not everyone who says to me, 'Lord, Lord,' will **enter the kingdom of heaven**, but only the one who does the will of my Father who is in heaven. Many will say to me on that day, 'Lord, Lord, did we not prophesy in your name and in your name drive out demons and in your name perform many miracles?' Then I will tell them plainly, 'I never knew you. Away from me, you evildoers!'

John 3:3-8: Jesus replied, "Very truly I tell you, **no one can see the kingdom of God** unless they are born again." "How can someone be born when they are old?" Nicodemus asked. "Surely they cannot enter a second time into their mother's womb to be born!" Jesus answered, "Very truly I tell you, **no one can enter the kingdom of God** unless they are born of water and the Spirit. Flesh gives birth to flesh, but the Spirit gives birth to spirit. You should not be surprised at my saying, 'You must be born again.' The wind blows wherever it pleases. You hear its sound, but you cannot tell where it comes from or where it is going. So it is with everyone born of the Spirit."

Acts 14:22b: "We must go through many hardships **to enter the kingdom of God**," they said.

Mark 12:33-34: To love him with all your heart, with all your understanding and with all your strength, and to love your neighbor as yourself is more important than all burnt offerings and sacrifices." When Jesus saw that he had answered wisely, he said to him, "**You are not far from the kingdom of God**." And from then on no one dared ask him any more questions.

Matthew 18:1-4: At that time the disciples came to Jesus and asked, "**Who, then, is the greatest in the kingdom of heaven?**" He called a little child to him, and placed the child among them. And he said: "Truly I tell you, unless you change and become like little children, **you will never enter the kingdom of heaven**. Therefore, whoever **takes the lowly position of this child is the greatest in the kingdom of heaven**.

Matthew 19:14: Jesus said, "Let the little children come to me, and do not hinder them, **for the kingdom of heaven belongs to such as these**." (See also Mark 10:14-15; Luke 18:16.)

Matthew 19:11-12: Jesus replied, "Not everyone can accept this word, but only those to whom it has been given. For there are eunuchs who were born that way, and there are eunuchs who have been made eunuchs by others – and there are those who choose to live like **eunuchs for the sake of the kingdom of heaven**. The one who can accept this should accept it."

Matthew 19:23-24: Then Jesus said to his disciples, "Truly I tell you, **it is hard for someone who is rich to enter the kingdom of heaven**. Again I tell you, it is easier for a camel to go through the eye of a needle than for **someone who is rich to enter the kingdom of God**." (See also Mark 10:23; Luke 18:18.)

Parable of the Wedding Feast – Matthew 22:1-14; Luke 14:16-24
Matthew 22:2-14: "**The kingdom of heaven is like** a king who prepared a wedding banquet for his son...' "For many are invited, but few are chosen."

Matthew 23:13: Woe to you, teachers of the law and Pharisees, you hypocrites! **You shut the door of the kingdom of heaven in people's faces.** You yourselves do not enter, nor will you let those enter who are trying to.

Parable of the Sheep and Goats –
Matthew 25:31-46: "When the Son of Man comes in his glory, and all the angels with him, he will sit on his glorious throne. All the nations will be gathered before him, and he will separate the people one from another as a shepherd separates the sheep from the goats. He will put the sheep on his right and the goats on his left. "Then the King will say to those on his right, 'Come, you who are blessed by my Father; **take your inheritance, the kingdom prepared for you since the creation of the world.** For I was hungry and you gave me something to eat, I was thirsty and you gave me something to drink, I was a stranger and you invited me in, I needed clothes and you clothed me, I was sick and you looked after me, I was in prison and you came to visit me.' ...

Mark 9:43-48: If your hand causes you to stumble, cut it off. It is **better for you to enter life [the Kingdom]** maimed than with two hands to go into hell, where the fire never goes out. ... And if your foot causes you to stumble, cut it off. It is **better for you to enter life [the Kingdom]** crippled than to have two feet and be thrown into hell. ... And if your eye causes you to stumble, pluck it out. It is **better for you to enter the kingdom of God** with one eye than to have two eyes and be thrown into hell, where 'the worms that eat them do not die, and the fire is not quenched.'

Luke 21:31: Even so, when you see these things happening, you know that **the kingdom of God is near.**

Matthew 10:37-39: Anyone who loves their father or mother more than me is **not worthy of me [my Kingdom]**; anyone who loves their son or daughter more than me is **not worthy of me [my Kingdom]**. Whoever does not take up their cross and follow me is **not worthy of me [my Kingdom]**. Whoever finds their life will lose it, and whoever loses their life for my sake will find it.

1 Corinthians 6:9-11: Or do you not know that **wrongdoers will not inherit the kingdom of God?** Do not be deceived: Neither the sexually immoral nor idolaters nor adulterers nor men who have sex with men nor thieves nor the greedy nor drunkards nor slanderers nor swindlers will **inherit the kingdom of God.** And that is what some of you were. But you were washed, you were sanctified, you were justified in the name of the Lord Jesus Christ and by the Spirit of our God.

1 Corinthians 15:48-50: As was the earthly man, so are those who are of the earth; and as is the heavenly man, so also are those who are of heaven. And just as we have borne the image of the earthly man, so shall we bear the image of the heavenly man. I declare to you, brothers and sisters, that **flesh and blood cannot inherit the kingdom of God**, nor does the perishable inherit the imperishable.

Galatians 5:19-21: The acts of the flesh are obvious: sexual immorality, impurity and debauchery; idolatry and witchcraft; hatred, discord, jealousy, fits of rage, selfish ambition, dissensions, factions and envy; drunkenness, orgies, and the like. I warn you, as I did before, that **those who live like this will not inherit the kingdom of God.**

Ephesians 5:5-6: For of this you can be sure: No immoral, impure or greedy person – such a person is an idolater – **has any inheritance in the kingdom of Christ and of God.** Let no one deceive you with empty words, for because of such things God's wrath comes on those who are disobedient.

Colossians 1:12-14: and giving joyful thanks to the Father, who has **qualified you to share in the inheritance of his holy people in the kingdom of light.** For he has rescued us from the dominion of darkness and **brought us into the kingdom of the Son he loves**, in whom we have redemption, the forgiveness of sins.

1 Thessalonians 2:11-12: For you know that we dealt with each of you as a father deals with his own children, encouraging, comforting and urging you to live lives worthy of God, **who calls you into his kingdom and glory.**

2 Thessalonians 1:4-5: Therefore, among God's churches we boast about your perseverance and faith in all the persecutions and trials you are enduring. All this is evidence that God's judgment is right, and as a result you will be **counted worthy of the kingdom of God, for which you are suffering**.

Hebrews 12:25-29: See to it that you do not refuse him who speaks. If they did not escape when they refused him who warned them on earth, how much less will we, if we turn away from him who warns us from heaven? At that time his voice shook the earth, but now he has promised, "Once more I will shake not only the earth but also the heavens." The words "once more" indicate the removing of what can be shaken – that is, created things – so that what cannot be shaken may remain. Therefore, **since we are receiving a kingdom that cannot be shaken**, let us be thankful, and so worship God acceptably with reverence and awe, for our "God is a consuming fire."

James 2:5: Listen, my dear brothers and sisters: Has not God chosen those who are poor in the eyes of the world to be rich in faith and to **inherit the kingdom** he promised those who love him?

2 Peter 1:10-11: Therefore, my brothers and sisters, make every effort to confirm your calling and election. For if you do these things, you will never stumble, and you will **receive a rich welcome into the eternal kingdom of our Lord and Savior Jesus Christ**.

Revelation 21:7-8: **Those who are victorious will inherit all this [the Kingdom]**, and I will be their God and they will be my children. But the cowardly, the unbelieving, the vile, the murderers, the sexually immoral, those who practice magic arts, the idolaters and all liars – they will be consigned to the fiery lake of burning sulfur. This is the second death."

John 14:6: Jesus answered, "I am the way and the truth and the life. **No one comes to the Father [into the Kingdom] except through me**.

Revelation 20:15: Anyone whose name was not found written in the book of life was thrown into the lake of fire [not the Kingdom].

Revelation 22:14-15: "Blessed are those who wash their robes, that they may have the right to the tree of life and **may go through the gates into the city [of the Kingdom.]** Outside are the dogs, those who practice magic arts, the sexually immoral, the murderers, the idolaters and everyone who loves and practices falsehood.

Galatians 6:7-8: Do not be deceived: God cannot be mocked. A man reaps what he sows. Whoever sows to please their flesh, from the flesh will reap destruction; whoever sows to please the Spirit, **from the Spirit will reap eternal life [in the Kingdom of God.]**

Every Day
BLESSINGS OF THE RIGHTEOUS

Habakkuk 2:4: Behold, his soul is puffed up; it is not upright within him, but **the righteous shall live by his faith**. (See also Galatians 3:11; Hebrews 10:38.)

Romans 1:16-17: For I am not ashamed of the gospel, because it is the power of God that brings salvation to everyone who believes: first to the Jew, then to the Gentile. For in the gospel the righteousness of God is revealed – a righteousness that is by faith from first to last, just as it is written: "**The righteous will live by faith.**"

2 Corinthians 5:21: God made him who had no sin to be sin for us, so that in him **we might become the righteousness of God**.

Psalm 112:1-10: Praise the LORD. **Blessed are those who fear the LORD**, who find great delight in his commands. Their children will be mighty in the land; the generation of the upright will be blessed. Wealth and riches are in their houses, and their righteousness endures forever. Even in darkness light dawns for the upright, for **those who are gracious and compassionate and righteous**. Good will come to those who are generous and lend freely, **who conduct their affairs with justice. Surely the righteous will never be shaken**; they will be remembered forever. They will have no fear of bad news; their hearts are steadfast, trusting in the LORD. Their hearts are secure, they will have no fear; in the end they will look in triumph on their foes. They have freely scattered their gifts to the poor, **their righteousness endures forever**; their horn will be lifted high in honor. The wicked will see and be vexed, they will gnash their teeth and waste away; the longings of the wicked will come to nothing.

Psalm 1:6: For the LORD watches over **the way of the righteous**, but the way of the wicked leads to destruction.

Psalm 5:12: Surely, LORD, **you bless the righteous**; you surround them with your favor as with a shield.

Psalm 11:4-7: The LORD is in his holy temple; the LORD is on his heavenly throne. He observes everyone on earth; his eyes examine them. **The LORD examines the righteous**, but the wicked, those who love violence, he hates with a passion. On the wicked he will rain fiery coals and burning sulfur; a scorching wind will be their lot. For the LORD is righteous, he loves justice; the upright will see his face.

Every Day: Blessings of the Righteous

Psalm 14:5: But there they are, overwhelmed with dread, for **God is present in the company of the righteous.**

Psalm 34:15-17, 19-22: **The eyes of the LORD are on the righteous**, and his ears are attentive to their cry; but the face of the LORD is against those who do evil, to blot out their name from the earth.... **The righteous cry out, and the LORD hears them**; he delivers them from all their troubles. ... **The righteous person may have many troubles, but the LORD delivers him from them all**; he protects all his bones, not one of them will be broken. ...Evil will slay the wicked; **the foes of the righteous will be condemned**. The LORD will rescue his servants; no one who takes refuge in him will be condemned.

Psalm 37:16-17, 21-26, 29-33, 39-40: **Better the little that the righteous have** than the wealth of many wicked; for the power of the wicked will be broken, but the LORD upholds the righteous. ... The wicked borrow and do not repay, but **the righteous give generously**; those the LORD blesses will inherit the land, but those he curses will be destroyed. **The LORD makes firm the steps of the one who delights in him**; though he may stumble, he will not fall, for the LORD upholds him with his hand. I was young and now I am old, yet **I have never seen the righteous forsaken or their children begging bread**. They are always generous and lend freely; their children will be a blessing. ... **The righteous will inherit the land and dwell in it forever. The mouths of the righteous utter wisdom, and their tongues speak what is just.** The law of their God is in their hearts; their feet do not slip. The wicked lie in wait for the righteous, intent on putting them to death; but the LORD will not leave them in the power of the wicked or let them be condemned when brought to trial. ... **The salvation of the righteous comes from the LORD; he is their stronghold in time of trouble.** The LORD helps them and delivers them; he delivers them from the wicked and saves them, because they take refuge in him.

Psalm 58:10-11: **The righteous will be glad when they are avenged**, when they dip their feet in the blood of the wicked. Then people will say, "**Surely the righteous still are rewarded**; surely there is a God who judges the earth."

Psalm 92:12-15: **The righteous will flourish like a palm tree**, they will grow like a cedar of Lebanon; planted in the house of the LORD, they will flourish in the courts of our God. They will still bear fruit in old age, they will stay fresh and green, proclaiming, "The LORD is upright; he is my Rock, and there is no wickedness in him."

Proverbs 10:3, 6, 16, 25, 28, 30: **The LORD does not let the righteous go hungry**, but he thwarts the craving of the wicked. ... Blessings crown the head of the righteous, but violence overwhelms the mouth of the wicked. ... **The wages of the righteous is life**, but the earnings of the wicked are sin and death. ... When the storm has swept by, the wicked are gone, **but the righteous stand firm forever**. ... **The prospect of the righteous is joy**, but the hopes of the wicked come to nothing. ... **The righteous will never be uprooted**, but the wicked will not remain in the land.

Proverbs 11:4, 8, 21, 30-31: Wealth is worthless in the day of wrath, **but righteousness delivers from death**. ... **The righteous person is rescued from trouble**, and it falls on the wicked instead. ... Be sure of this: The wicked will not go unpunished, but **those who are righteous will go free. ... The fruit of the righteous is a tree of life**, and the one who is wise saves lives. **If the righteous receive their due on earth**, how much more the ungodly and the sinner! Proverbs 15:6, 29: **The house of the righteous contains great treasure**, but the income of the wicked brings ruin. ... The LORD is far from the wicked, **but he hears the prayer of the righteous.**

1 John 3:7-8: Dear children, do not let anyone lead you astray. **The one who does what is right is righteous, just as he is righteous.** The one who does what is sinful is of the devil, because the devil has been sinning from the beginning. The reason the Son of God appeared was to destroy the devil's work.

Every Day
THE BRIDE OF CHRIST

Ephesians 5:22-32: Wives, submit to your own husbands, as to the Lord. For the husband is the head of the wife even as Christ is the head of the church, his body, and is himself its Savior. Now as the church submits to Christ, so also wives should submit in everything to their husbands. Husbands, love your wives, **as Christ loved the church and gave himself up for her, that he might sanctify her, having cleansed her by the washing of water with the word, so that he might present the church to himself in splendor, without spot or wrinkle or any such thing, that she might be holy and without blemish.** In the same way husbands should love their wives as their own bodies. **He who loves his wife loves himself. For no one ever hated his own flesh, but nourishes and cherishes it, just as Christ does the church, because we are members of his body.** "Therefore a man shall leave his father and mother and hold fast to his wife, and the two shall become one flesh." **This mystery is profound, and I am saying that it refers to Christ and the church.**

Genesis 2:22-25: And the rib that the LORD God had taken from the man he made into a woman and brought her to the man. Then the man said, "This at last is bone of my bones and flesh of my flesh; she shall be called Woman, because she was taken out of Man." Therefore a man shall leave his father and his mother and hold fast to his wife, and they shall become one flesh. And the man and his wife were both naked and were not ashamed.

2 Corinthians 11:2-4: For I feel a divine jealousy for you, since **I betrothed you to one husband, to present you as a pure virgin to Christ.** But I am afraid that as the serpent deceived Eve by his cunning, your thoughts will be led astray from a sincere and pure devotion to Christ. For if someone comes and proclaims another Jesus than the one we proclaimed, or if you receive a different spirit from the one you received, or if you accept a different gospel from the one you accepted, you put up with it readily enough.

Revelation 19:6-9: Then I heard what seemed to be the voice of a great multitude, like the roar of many waters and like the sound of mighty peals of thunder, crying out, "Hallelujah! For the Lord our God the Almighty reigns. Let us rejoice and exult and give him the glory, **for the marriage of the Lamb has come, and his Bride has made herself ready; it was granted her to clothe herself with fine linen, bright and pure" – for the fine linen is the righteous deeds of the saints.** And the angel said to me, "Write this: **Blessed are those who are invited to the marriage supper of the Lamb.**" And he said to me, "These are the true words of God."

Revelation 21:2-4: And I saw the holy city, new Jerusalem, coming down out of heaven from God, **prepared as a bride adorned for her husband.** And I heard a loud voice from the throne saying, "Behold, the dwelling place of God is with man. He will dwell with them, and they will be his people, and God himself will be with them as their God. He will wipe away every tear from their eyes, and death shall be no more, neither shall there be mourning, nor crying, nor pain anymore, for the former things have passed away."...

Revelation 21:9-11: Then came one of the seven angels who had the seven bowls full of the seven last plagues and spoke to me, saying, "**Come, I will show you the Bride, the wife of the Lamb**." And he carried me away in the Spirit to a great, high mountain, and showed me the holy city Jerusalem coming down out of heaven from God, having the glory of God, its radiance like a most rare jewel, like a jasper, clear as crystal...

Revelation 22:17: **The Spirit and the Bride** say, "Come." And let the one who hears say, "Come." And let the one who is thirsty come; let the one who desires take the water of life without price.

Isaiah 54:4-8: "Fear not, for you will not be ashamed; be not confounded, for you will not be disgraced; for you will forget the shame of your youth, and the reproach of your widowhood you will remember no more. **For your Maker is your husband, the LORD of hosts is his name**; and the Holy One of Israel is your Redeemer, the God of the whole earth he is called. For the LORD has called you like a wife deserted and grieved in spirit, like a wife of youth when she is cast off, says your God. For a brief moment I deserted you, but with great compassion I will gather you. In overflowing anger for a moment I hid my face from you, but with everlasting love I will have compassion on you," says the LORD, your Redeemer... [continues]

Isaiah 62:3-5: You shall be a crown of beauty in the hand of the LORD, and a royal diadem in the hand of your God. You shall no more be termed Forsaken, and your land shall no more be termed Desolate, **but you shall be called My Delight Is in Her [Hephzibah], and your land Married [Beulah]; for the LORD delights in you, and your land shall be married**. For as a young man marries a young woman, so shall your sons marry you, and **as the bridegroom rejoices over the bride, so shall your God rejoice over you**.

Hosea 2:14-20: "Therefore, behold, I will allure her, and bring her into the wilderness, and speak tenderly to her. And there I will give her her vineyards and make the Valley of Achor a door of hope. And there she shall answer as in the days of her youth, as at the time when she came out of the land of Egypt. "**And in that day, declares the LORD, you will call me 'My Husband,'** and no longer will you call me 'My Baal.' For I will remove the names of the Baals from her mouth, and they shall be remembered by name no more. And I will make for them a covenant on that day with the beasts of the field, the birds of the heavens, and the creeping things of the ground. And I will abolish the bow, the sword, and war from the land, and I will make you lie down in safety. **And I will betroth you to me forever. I will betroth you to me in righteousness and in justice, in steadfast love and in mercy. I will betroth you to me in faithfulness**. And you shall know the LORD.

Jeremiah 2:2: "Go and proclaim in the hearing of Jerusalem, Thus says the LORD, "I remember the devotion of your youth, **your love as a bride**, how you followed me in the wilderness, in a land not sown... [continues]

Ezekiel 16:8-14: "When I passed by you again and saw you, behold, you were at the age for love, and I spread the corner of my garment over you and covered your nakedness; I made my vow to you and **entered into a covenant with you, declares the Lord GOD, and you became mine**. Then I bathed you with water and washed off your blood from you and anointed you with oil. I clothed you also with embroidered cloth and shod you with fine leather. I wrapped you in fine linen and covered you with silk. And I adorned you with ornaments and put bracelets on your wrists and a chain on your neck. And I put a ring on your nose and earrings in your ears and a beautiful crown on your head. Thus you were adorned with gold and silver, and your clothing was of fine linen and silk and embroidered cloth. You ate fine flour and honey and oil. You grew exceedingly beautiful and advanced to royalty. And your renown went forth among the nations because of your beauty, for it was perfect through the splendor that I had bestowed on you, declares the Lord GOD... [continues]

Mark 2:18-22: Now John's disciples and the Pharisees were fasting. And people came and said to him, "Why do John's disciples and the disciples of the Pharisees fast, but your disciples do not fast?" And Jesus said to them, "**Can the wedding guests fast while the bridegroom is with them? As long as they have the bridegroom with them, they cannot fast. The days will come when the bridegroom is taken away from them, and then they will fast in that day**. No one sews a piece of unshrunk cloth on an old garment. If he does, the patch tears away from it, the new from the old, and a worse tear is made. And no one puts new wine into old wineskins. If he does, the wine will burst the skins – and the wine is destroyed, and so are the skins. But new wine is for fresh wineskins." (See also Matthew 9:15.)

John 3:29-30: **The one who has the bride is the bridegroom**. The friend of the bridegroom, who stands and hears him, rejoices greatly at the bridegroom's voice. Therefore this joy of mine is now complete. He must increase, but I must decrease."

ABOUT THE AUTHOR

Wendy Bowen has lived entirely by faith for many years in the *literal* application of what is today known as the Manifest International Approach, (see manifestinternational.com/approach) God has never failed her. She proclaims Jesus, the whole counsel of God, and spreads the message of God's faithfulness all over the world. She equips followers of Jesus to live by faith in these end-times so as to endure to the end and be saved.

ABOUT MANIFEST INTERNATIONAL

We exist to reveal Jesus, proclaim His Kingdom, and equip His disciples for spiritual maturity and ministry. We live by faith and allow Jesus to lead, guide, and transform every aspect of our lives for His glory. We live to manifest our King to the world until He returns.

www.manifestinternational.com

Manifest
INTERNATIONAL
We Live to Manifest Our King

www.ingramcontent.com/pod-product-compliance
Lightning Source LLC
Chambersburg PA
CBHW080444110426
42743CB00016B/3269